W9-AUA-063

Keep Your LIGHTS On

To Larry LaDuke

8.6.2010

Keep Your LIGHTS On

Learn the art of staying
focused,
encouraged,
and enthused
about your personal and
career goals.

Tom Gunnels

Introduction by John Powell

ThomasMore®
– An RCL Company –
Allen, Texas

Front Cover Design by James Ward, WaveBase 9

Copyright 1998 Tom Gunnels

All rights reserved. No part of this book shall be reproduced or transmitted in any form or by any means, electronic or mechanical, including photocopying, recording, or by any information or retrieval system, without written permission from the Publisher.

Send all inquiries to:
Thomas More® Publishing
An RCL Company
200 East Bethany Drive
Allen, Texas 75002-3804

Toll Free 800-264-0368
Fax 800-688-8356

Printed in the United States of America

ISBN 0-88347-404-2

1 2 3 4 5 02 01 00 99 98

Contents

Dedication

Among my richest blessings are the people in my balcony. They believed in me so strongly that I wanted to be what they could see in me. To all of them I proudly dedicate *Keep Your Lights On.*

Cecil F. Adam (1909–1995)

W.W. Billips

Jean Dietz

Frankie Regas Gunnels

Sue Lee Gunnels (1934–1965)

T.P. Gunnels (1897–1977)

George Pope

Katharine Street (1908–1988)

To our four wonderful grandchildren:

Matt Terrill, Melissa Terrill, Lauren Harville, and Conner Harville

Success is not the result of spontaneous combustion.
You must set yourself on fire.

—Author unknown

Acknowledgments

Keep Your Lights On is the result of great faith and encouragement that came from many sources. Foremost among them is Frankie. She has kept my lights burning brightly since we married in 1970. Frankie's suggestions, encouragement and conviction are vital to my work. She is my helpful critic and my staunch supporter, a powerful combination.

Serving on the board of the Tom Gunnels Seminars Company are Andy Anderson and Charles Hartsell. Each Tuesday, we met to critique my prior week's work. Their suggestions helped to shape the manuscript and fine-tune the core messages. Two other directors are daughters Susan Terrill and Sandra Harville. They offered creative ideas incorporated in the finished product.

My 41-year career with the State Farm Insurance Companies provided an incredible array of fulfilling and enriching experiences. In that career, I worked with some great insurance professionals that gave me the foundation for *Keep Your Lights On*. I am privileged to have been a part of State Farm, one of the world's greatest business organizations.

Debra Hampton's work as the managing editor is a rare gift. To our partnership she brought a sense of excellence and consistency of messages that improved the focus of my writing. A huge measure of the book's success will be the result of her creative guidance and suggestions.

Mitzi Carpenter is my invaluable administrative assistant. She did proofing while offering suggestions and insights that strengthened my messages.

John Powell's outstanding books have taken me on a journey of self-improvement that eventually led to *Keep Your Lights On*. I've recommended his work to audiences across the United States and Canada. Visiting with him at Loyola University is one of my personal high-water marks.

Keep Your Lights On introduces the people in my "balcony." They are responsible for propelling me on my journey to meet Tom Gunnels. Without them, *Keep Your Lights On* could not exist.

I am proof that no one walks alone. At many stages in my life, I was touched by people who pointed the way for my journey. It's been a great trip so far. More challenges and excitement lie ahead. As John Powell tells his university students, I also say, "The Lord is not through with me yet, so be gentle." More remains for me to do. I give thanks to all who encourage me to get it done. When we meet, I pray that we will know each other by the brightness of our lights.

—Tom Gunnels

Introduction

My first acquaintance with Tom Gunnels was in the form of a letter Tom wrote me: He asked me to intercede for him and to request an interview with Johnny Carson, who at that time was host of the *Late Show.* "Ask him to have this Tennessee boy on his show," Tom requested.

The next meeting was a person-to-person encounter in my office. Tom asked many questions and listened intently to my answers. He asked about presenting his *Keep Your Lights On* philosophy in book form. After learning a little of the contents, I did what I could to encourage him. I was able to direct him to Thomas More, which has published all of my books.

Then, the manuscript for this book was sent to me. I was surprised at how well "this Tennessee boy" writes. Everything seemed very clear to me. There were no difficult sentences. No need to look up words.

Self-revelation is said to be a high-risk form of writing. I have asked myself, "What is the high risk?" I am now convinced that it is twofold: 1) It is highly emotional, and many readers generally can't stand the sight of blood. 2) It also runs the risk of sounding like "tooting your own horn."

Something about the way Tom Gunnels does it seems to avoid both of these risks, as I see it. He shares of himself, both the successes of his life as well as the tragedies. He tells of his self-celebration as well as the deaths of his mother and his first wife.

I was particularly taken with Tom's description of "the people in his balcony," and "liking oneself." I was also very impressed by the fact that Tom suggests lists and letters-to-be-written to the reader. It has been said: "You can always tell a teacher, but you can't tell them much." I know from long experience in the classroom that the work students do on their own is much more valuable than the lectures and texts.

And if anyone has doubts about the ability of human beings to change, witness the self-described change in this author.

In the words of the U.S. Army commercial: "Be all you can be." Irenaeus wrote in the second century: "The glory of God is a person who is fully alive." In the words of Tom Gunnels: "Keep Your Lights On."

—John Powell

(John Powell is the best-selling author of 19 books that have sold more than 15 million copies, including *Why Am I Afraid to Tell You Who I Am?* and *Solving the Riddle of Self.*)

Foreword

Early in my adult life, I observed three things about those who accomplished more and moved to the top of their professions: (1) they focus on what they are doing; (2) they keep encouraging themselves; and (3) they maintain their enthusiasm. I made a conscious decision to emulate those attitudes and began a quest that has led me to this book, *Keep Your Lights On*.

Originally developed as a special event program featured throughout the United States and in Canada, *Keep Your Lights On* teaches the art of staying focused, encouraged, and enthused on personal and professional goals that are important to you.

Whenever I talk to outstandingly successful business people, such as Sam Beall, founder of the Ruby Tuesday Restaurant Chain, I ask them to define their formula for success. Like so many others, Mr. Beall says that his three secrets are "focus, focus, focus."

When we lose focus in any endeavor—business, family, sports—we don't do our best. As an amateur tennis player, I know that when I lose focus, I lose the game. The same result occurs in all other areas of human endeavor: When we lose focus, we lose.

Keep Your Lights On adds two elements beyond focus: staying encouraged and being enthused. If your goal is to make it to the top—in all facets of your life—you must pay the fee. And what is that fee? You must keep the focus, stay encouraged, and be enthused. Keep your lights on! No matter what!

My favorite sports hero is Jerry Rice of the San Francisco Forty-Niners. The fact that he is outstandingly successful, owning virtually every NFL record for his position, is just one reason. The fact that he started poor and rose to prominence is but another. His dedication to being prepared to play on game day is a trademark I applaud.

The main reason I admire Rice so much is that he recognizes and accepts that he is a role model for millions of our young people and conducts his life accordingly. I love his statement: "God gave me some abilities to play football. I think God wants me to play the best football I can." Thank you, Jerry Rice, for striving to set a positive example for all of us, whether or not we are football fans.

Whatever abilities God gave Jerry Rice or Tom Gunnels or you, I believe God intends that we put our abilities to the best possible use. Otherwise, why bother to bless us with these gifts? When I hear people say that they are not particularly gifted, I assume they are expressing how they really feel about themselves. (You will learn that I have been there!)

The fact is that how these people feel about themselves is probably not based on truth or reality. I've never met a person who had an accurate, unbiased assessment of his or her attributes and abilities. Few of us see ourselves in all our glory. We wear blinders that keep us from seeing ourselves at our best. Our inability to see ourselves in our fullness robs us—and the world—of the opportunity to be all that God designed us to be. We are more than we realize.

My work in this arena was born out of my desire to rise to the top of my profession and to be "fully alive" as a husband, parent, church worker, and citizen in my community. I wanted to know the real me. I didn't want to hold back anything that could contribute to my personal and professional growth and attainment.

This book provides the story of my quest to stay focused, to encourage myself, and to maintain enthusiasm for my life. I present this information to help you recognize similar truths about yourself.

As you read the following chapters, you will learn that at times, my "lights" are off. What do I do then? I follow a few simple principles that help me get them back on. These principles can help you as well. God put certain "lights"—abilities, attributes and gifts—inside each of us. But these lights do not rise to the surface of our life on their own. It's up to us, individually, to get those lights shining brightly, for our own benefit and for those who will follow our path.The greatest economic tragedy in the world is that we can choose to live below our potential. Yet, we need not. When we hold ourselves to a higher standard, we raise the bar for those who are observing us. As they note our actions, they conclude that the way we act is *the* way *to* act. And so, they, too, realize their potential. We become their beacon of hope. Our light shines before them.

Are you ready to begin a journey that you likely will never complete but that you will always be glad you began? If so, I bid you welcome. You are joining a select group of people determined to discover their best.

If you're ready for great things to happen, they will. Hold onto your resolve. The ride may be somewhat bumpy, but the longer you persist in your journey, the smoother the path becomes. The brighter your lights burn, the clearer the road and the greater progress you will make. Hold on to your dreams. You are about to take a giant step in discovering a you who is far greater than you ever imagined. You are in charge. No one else has the power to discover the real you. What you do will be by your intention. Nothing will be accidental, but by your design a better, brighter you will emerge.

Is this too much to expect? No, not if you are willing to become accountable for yourself. I say this because one of the tenets for personal growth is that we must accept responsibility for who we are, where we are, and where we are going. There's no free lunch. We must pay for what we get and accept responsibility for what we have done, for what we are doing, and for what we will do and be.

According to an ancient saying, "If the student is ready, the teacher can teach." Now that you've made the decision to become a student there is more about you that you want to uncover. Good! We are ready to start. Let us begin! And let us acknowledge that we can't be a beacon for others, if our lights don't shine!

Starting the Journey

1

Compelling Challenges

What are the three most compelling challenges you face in the current decade? I've asked thousands of people throughout the United States and Canada to answer that question. Their collective responses offer you helpful insights as you seek a greater vision of yourself and as you prepare to use your talents and opportunities to their fullest.

The similarity of the responses has been absolutely amazing. The top three remain the same whether the members of the group to whom I am speaking are in their teens or their 60s; whether they are business owners or clerks; college or high school students; Eagle Scouts or Tenderfoots; high income earners or those just getting started. The answers from each group follow the same pattern. Further, the responses reveal no gender differences. From this similarity of response, I have concluded that all God's children encounter similar struggles.

This has been a revelation to me. During most of my adult life I thought I was the only person who really had to struggle to keep focused, encouraged, and enthused. Now I know that I am not alone, that I fight the same battles as everyone else. You may find, as I have, a renewal of strength and purpose in the knowledge that your friends and neighbors share the same basic challenges that you encounter each day.

THE THREE MOST COMPELLING CHALLENGES

After asking thousands of individuals in the United States and Canada "What are your three most compelling challenges?" I tallied their responses and discovered the following:

- The primary concern for 81 percent of the respondents was staying focused, encouraged, and enthused. They let themselves down by feeling scattered, discouraged, and apathetic about their life and work. They wanted "to keep their lights on," but somehow couldn't always do this.

- For 79 percent of the respondents, a financial issue was one of their three major concerns. Often this issue had to do with funding their children's college education, preparing for their own retirement, or meeting some major financial urgency within the family.

- For 47 percent, one of their three major personal concerns involved their family: a divorce, a death, or a disability. The respondents also frequently noted a hunger to find a balance between their professional and their personal lives.
- For 33 percent, personal health was an important concern—overcoming an illness or developing improved habits to enhance their own well-being.
- For 12 percent, government intervention in their professional lives was an issue.
- For 6 percent, the public's perception of their profession worried them.
- Another 6 percent listed as their concerns spiritual growth, a desire for better office organization, greater drug prevention, and worries about rearing their children properly.

(Note that the total of these percentages does not equal 300 because some respondents listed all three concerns in one category, such as staying focused, encouraged, and enthused.)

Knowing our concerns gives us a compass to chart a new course toward a more meaningful and rewarding future. For this life isn't a dress rehearsal; it's the real thing. So we must keep our lights shining brightly. When we do this, we light our own way. We also become a beacon for those who are following us. We help them walk their own paths more easily. (Yes, there are people, often those whom we'd least suspect, who are watching each one of us and concluding that whatever we are doing and whatever we are not doing is the right way to do things.)

How do we begin to find our best selves on this journey? How do we stay focused, encouraged, enthused? Scott Peck began his world-famous book *The Road Less Traveled* with the words "Life is difficult." Most of us would agree with him. But in the midst of difficulty, most of us also want meaning. We want our life to count for something. We want to tap into our inner resources, the "lights" within us, and become a beacon for others.

FIVE TRUTHS FOR YOUR JOURNEY

Throughout a management career that has spanned 41 years, I have been privileged to work with many outstandingly successful business people. As we became more open with one another, all of us learned five things:

(1) Each of us had to intentionally work at staying positive.

(2) Each of us, at times, felt discouraged and unable to meet the commitments of the day.

(3) When we developed upbeat expectations, we got upbeat results. Conversely, when

we let our perceptions become negative, we met only undesirable results.

(4) Each of us had more abilities than we had previously thought.

(5) Our willingness to challenge our own perceptions, whatever the origin, always brought dramatic growth in the area confronted. The search for a better way required us to be open to new information, insights and understanding—to challenge our own perceptions.

You have probably already discovered these five truths for yourself. If you desire a journey to find the best you—in all areas of you life—then here is a place to begin. Welcome these truths within your life. But know this up front: While this journey requires great tenacity and an inordinate amount of inner courage, you'll never regret having started it, even if you do not reach the destination you set for yourself. In the midst of the journey, you may discover that a side road leads to a new goal that will fulfill your deepest desires.

Excited? If not now, you will be soon. Your best, like mine, is ahead. As we light the way for ourselves, we light the way for one another. Together, we help one another walk in the light and we keep one another from stumbling.

Keeping your lights on is an art. I can teach it; you can learn it. I know, because I have been both teacher and learner. And believe me, you, too, will become both teacher and learner to those you meet during your lifetime.

We have much work to do. The rewards are huge; the risk is small. The only way to lose is to not start.

If you want to start keeping your lights on, complete Worksheet 1 on pages 28–29. Remember: what you answer today may not be what you would answer in a decade or two or in a year or two or even in a month or two. You are not writing in concrete; you can change your mind. So feel free to think only of the concerns that occupy you today.

Letter from "Keep Your Lights On" Seminar

Jonathan, my 12-year-old son, and I attended your KYLO presentation. The next day Jonathan pitched his first no-hitter. When I asked what he had done differently, he said, "I remembered what Mr. Gunnels said about staying focused, staying encouraged, and staying enthused."

Carl W. Gjeldum
Naperville, Ill.

KEEP YOUR LIGHTS ON BY DOING THE FOLLOWING:

1. Remember that your personal challenges are like those of others.
2. To begin to meet your challenges, identify them.
3. Understand that when you keep your lights on, you help yourself walk without stumbling and you light the way for others.
4. To make your life meaningful, tap into your inner resources and release the lights within so that they become a beacon for others.
5. Be assured that keeping your lights on is an art that you can both learn and teach.

WORKSHEET 1
THE CONCERNS OF MY PRESENT LIFE

Please review the topics listed below and mark your top three concerns and challenges for this year. Mark only three out of the entire list. If the worksheet does not list your three top concerns and challenges, please write them under the "other concerns" category.

Financial, Personal, and Business

1. _____ Keep Income Growing
2. _____ Be Financially Secure
3. _____ Finance College Education
4. _____ Finance Retirement

Marketing

5. _____ Upgrade My Market
6. _____ Get Enough Clients
7. _____ Improve Marketing Techniques

Staying Encouraged and Focused

8. _____ Stay Enthusiastic
9. _____ Improve Professionally
10. _____ Establish Better Time Management
11. _____ Maintain Positive Attitudes
12. _____ Create a Better Vision of Myself
13. _____ Remain Focused on Career Goals
14. _____ Achieve Personal Goals

Health Issues

15. _____ Keep/Develop Good Health Habits
16. _____ Overcome Personal Health Problems

Government Issues

17. _____ Avoid Government Intervention

Public Perspective Issues

18. _____ Determine How the Public Views Me

Family Issues

19. _____ Find Enough Time for Family
20. _____ Create a Better Balance in My Life
21. _____ Be More Supportive of My Family's Concerns

Other Concerns

List any concerns and challenges that the 21 items above do not enumerate.

22. ______________________________
23. ______________________________
24. ______________________________

____

Date you completed this survey

2

The Celebration

The instructions are clear. If the Church of the Ascension Episcopal won't allow it, then the Bearden Baptist Church will be asked. If neither says yes, then an auditorium at one of the high schools or a theater will do just fine. Where is not as important as how and what. There can be no exception, no roadblocks, to the how and what. My outline is specific and clear.

In this instance, however, after much ecclesiastical wrangling and posturing, the rector at Ascension (yes, he consulted with the bishop several times!) grants permission to my family, primarily because of the persistency of my wife, Frankie. The "program of services" may proceed as designed.

"It's never been done this way," the rector says, "and it is definitely not Episcopal. However, we'll allow it." Reluctant approval, but still the service will be done "in accord with 'the outline.'" (That's how it came to be referenced—the outline.)

HPV Video's Danny Harb is in charge of setting up and operating the sound equipment. Crouch's Florist has prepared the floral arrangements on each side of the altar—a vivid collection of spring flowers, each containing one prominent red rose. (The flower represents the single red rose Frankie carried when we married.)

The chefs of Regas Restaurant have prepared a variety of delicacies to serve to the guests. Like the church, Regas has not done this before, but the restaurant manager is unable to decline Frankie's request. In the Regas tradition, the banquet will be done with grace and excellence.

The local news media, including the editors of the *Knoxville News Sentinel* and the *Metro Pulse* plus reporters from each of the three local TV stations, are well represented. (Ultimately, all of them reported that they had not previously covered an event quite like this one and that it was properly called a "celebration.")

The Ascension's music director knows his responsibilities well because Frankie went over the outline with him at least three times, "just to make sure everyone knows his assignment and the what, where and when." She has had the outline professionally printed. (In fact, the Printing Edge called in its crew over the weekend to get the outline done on time and up to standard.)

Each person, upon arrival at the church, receives a program. (Later they'll show it to their family and friends.) The choir has rehearsed and is robed and eager to perform some new music. The priests have studied their assignments carefully and are wearing their most colorful vestments. The organist, one of the best in the nation, is at the ready. And Frankie and the priests have briefed the cross, candle, and flag bearers. They know exactly what they are to do.

THE PROGRAM OF SERVICES BEGINS!

The trumpeter walks to the front of the choir loft, raises his horn and, with gusto, sounds the clarion call to signal that the celebration is to begin. To the beautiful strains of *Amazing Grace,* the procession begins to walk from the back of the church, down the center aisle to the altar. The cross, candle, and flag bearers lead; the priests follow; then the choir members.

The group called "family members" is next. Frankie is first. Our grandchildren—Matt, Melissa, Lauren, and Conner—walk with her. Behind them are my two daughters and their husbands: Susan and Ben; Sandra and Lacy. Next are my brothers and sister and their families and a gracious assortment of nieces, nephews, in-laws and their families. These all form the family group.

The next group is the Men's Bible Study Class; then all active and retired State Farm agents and claims personnel. Completing the honored members of the processional are representatives of several tennis groups: the Monday evening 6 P.M. group; the Tuesday 4 P.M. group; the Wednesday 6 P.M. group; the Thursday 4 P.M. group; and the Saturday tennis luncheon round table bunch.

(The latter is more correctly called a bunch, definitely not a group. Only the solemnity of the day keeps them from their customary wisecracks and the insulting of each other, one of their rich traditions.) Everyone attending feels a little anxious because no one is sure of all that will follow. Some, particularly the older Episcopalians, even wonder if this is the "right" thing to be doing. (The program will be different. Not weird, but different. However, when it is finished, all will be glad to have been present and to have participated.)

The rector goes to the pulpit and reads the assigned scriptures. He then makes the following announcement: "This may not be the last time this kind of service is conducted in an Episcopal Church, but likely it is the first. I am to explain that there will be moments when it will be appropriate for laughter, other times for tears, and always a time for prayer and joy. All are invited to receive the Lord's Supper. Following our service, everyone is invited to join the family in the parish hall where food and drink will be served and where the celebration will continue. The Regas Restaurant is catering the food today by special request."

One Daughter Celebrates My Life

The rector then retires to a place behind the altar. A hush falls on the crowd as Susan, my elder daughter, walks to the piano that has been placed in the nave, in front of the altar rail. Speaking into the microphone she says, "My dad loved each of us. He also loved Knoxville and Tennessee and, yes, he loved Big Orange football. Both of his daughters were born here, where he spent more than 40 years of his life, where he married Frankie, and where he experienced some of his greatest joys. Sorrows, well, he would say that there were a few. He would suggest we remember his mountain tops and not his valleys. And that is exactly what we are going to do today.

"Music touched my dad as it has touched all of us. There are songs that marked our special occasions. My dad has asked me to play two songs that signify memorable events in his life. The first is *The Impossible Dream,* dedicated to Frankie, our mom. It is their song.

"Dad and Frankie claimed *The Impossible Dream* as their song when they were dating. They danced to it under the stars in the Virgin Islands on their honeymoon. This song always brought tears of remembered joy, and it renewed their determination to always seek the magic in the moment. And they found the magic they sought. It is a song for all lovers, for the young at heart. My Dad hoped that for us today, *The Impossible Dream* will evoke memories of special moments in our honored relationships."

Susan begins to play. My daughter is a talented musician. (I am inclined to say gifted, but she has spent many years developing this talent.) On this day, more than any other, she wants her music to have the same passion, the same feeling she has in her heart. And so it does, bringing misty eyes to Frankie and members of our family.

When Susan finishes the song, she says, "My dad chose this song today to honor Frankie as his impossible dream. I'd like to quote for you the opening lines of a poem my dad wrote to Frankie on one of their anniversaries: 'She took a heart that barely beat and made it vibrate once more; she took a closed and darkened room and opened wide the sunshine door.' My mother loves that poem as one of Dad's treasured gifts to her."

Susan pauses to collect herself, then continues. "You may be surprised to learn that for most of his life my dad had two left feet. But on the night he married Frankie, at their wedding reception, he was able to feel for the first time the beat of the music. It was then that he was able to dance to that beat.

"Dad kept dancing the rest of his life. He asked me to play today *The Tennessee Waltz* as a reminder for each of us to keep dancing, no matter what. Keep dancing. When your feet can no longer dance, keep dancing in your mind and in your heart."

Few in the audience have ever heard *The Tennessee Waltz* performed so beautifully. The melodious strains, played so lovingly by my daughter, create one of the proud moments of the day. When the final note sounds, Susan sits quietly at the piano, permitting the listeners to savor the music. Then, gracefully, she rises, looks toward Frankie for a nod of approval and rejoins the family—poised, proud, and pleased. The mood has been set for all that is to follow.

ANOTHER DAUGHTER CONTINUES THE CELEBRATION

Next, Sandra, my younger daughter, walks to the microphone placed at the center of the nave. For just a moment she stands there, not saying a word. Then she begins to speak. Her voice is strong, resolute, passionate. "My dad really loved to play tennis. He said that the only reason he didn't play more tennis was because more people didn't ask him to play. Some of our great father-daughter special moments were spent on the tennis court.

"Dad also introduced tennis to each one of his four grandchildren. If they don't already know it, those grandchildren will someday realize that they won because granddad wanted them to win. He felt that teaching his grandsons and granddaughters the joy of playing and of winning was one of his proud duties.

"There were times, when we were just starting to play, that he would play the doubles court while we played the singles. As we progressed, however, he no longer gave us that advantage.

"My dad and I cherished our times together, whatever we were doing, but in tennis we could each go out and play our very best; give each other our best shot; and rejoice, no matter who won. I would chide him if he was not playing up to his potential.

"Among the valuable lessons I learned from my dad, two came from tennis: First, there is real joy in winning when you have given the game your best.

Second, when you have given your best, you can rejoice in the other guy winning. Those lessons also apply to other dimensions of our life as well. Since we cannot always win, obviously we enhance our enjoyment if we can learn to celebrate when the other person wins.

"My dad believed we should be active in our community and in our places of worship. He expressed that belief by his involvement in all dimensions of his life. For more than 20 years, he was the adult Sunday School Class convener. He also worked on search committees and took leadership roles and did fundraising.

"Dad also became involved in his community and three different organizations honored him with the equivalent of the 'man of the year' award. A listing of the organizations that he served as either president or chairman of the board includes Toastmasters Clubs—on four separate occasions; the We're Glad You're Here Campaign for the Knoxville Chamber; the Convention Bureau of the Knoxville Chamber; the Better Business Bureau; the National Conference of Christians and Jews; the General Agency Managers Association; and the Knoxville Association of Life Underwriters.

"Few people ever loved their work as my dad did. Born poor, he found through his work the opportunity to pull himself up by his bootstraps and to help others do the same. He never planned to retire, never even liked to talk about that possibility.

"Dad treasured his 41 years with the State Farm Insurance Companies where he was recognized and rewarded for his achievements. He copyrighted some of the concepts he developed at State Farm and used them for the Tom Gunnels Seminar Company, which he started the first day after his retirement from State Farm.

"Dad's core philosophy was 'Each one of us is in charge of who we are, where we are, and where we are going.' That became the focus of a special presentation he developed called 'Keep Your Lights On.' That saying defines the art of staying focused, encouraged, and enthused on goals important to you. He presented this program all over the United States and in Canada.

"Dad designed a special lapel pin with KYLO on it. The license plate on his car has KYLO on it. He had sports caps produced with his KYLO logo. But more importantly, his life has KYLO stamped all over it! You will not be surprised to know that one of my dad's favorite poems goes like this: 'It is better by far to light one little candle . . .'

"My dad's life reminds all of us that we are responsible for our own candle. But God also calls us to help those whose candles may be temporarily dim or blown out. He believed that no candle should stay out long. Among the plaques presented to my dad, one he particularly cherished was presented to him in Chicago by a State Farm group to whom he had presented a weeklong seminar. That plaque was entitled 'The Lamplighter.' It reads as follows:

He has taken his bright candle and is gone;
Into another room I cannot find,

But anyone can tell where he has been
By all the little lights he has left behind.

If you want to find where my dad has been, just follow the lights.

He left his lights on."

Sandra concludes by saying, "My dad sought always to live his life by keeping his lights on. As one of his very proud daughters, I can tell you that his lights stayed on sometimes under difficult circumstances. He always pointed out that keeping our lights on is an art, one that can be taught and learned. Dad knew that because he did both: he learned and he taught.

"Then, through teaching, he learned more and so had more to teach and thence, more to learn. I know my dad would want me to tell you that whatever we might claim for him is not nearly as important as what we decide to claim for ourselves."

Sandra pauses and then adds, "Unless we make our personal commitment to keep our own lights on and to become a beacon to those who are surely modeling themselves after us, unless we truly care whether we help someone else's lights stay bright, then my dad's lights will have lost much of their luster.

"My children and my sister and her children and our mother and I have decided to keep our lights on and to be beacons for others. My dad preached that to do otherwise than to keep our lights on would make us a victim of our own darkness. I share this with you, and my family and I encourage you to choose light."

Sandra has done her assignment well. Without a word, save a barely audible "Amen," she rejoins her family.

My Grandchildren Celebrate, Too

Then Matt, my eldest grandchild, walks to the microphone. For him, poise came early in his life, and he displays it today. He faces the audience, takes a deep breath, and says, "I speak for all four grandchildren. All four of us have our own stories to tell, but you would find one theme in all of them. Our granddad told each one us often that he was the luckiest granddad in the world. We knew, of course, that we were the luckiest grandchildren in the world, and we told him so.

"Now my Aunt Sandra tells me that all those years I was beating my granddad in tennis he was letting me win to teach me the joy of winning. Well, it worked, because I *do* enjoy winning!

"About the time I turned 13, I noticed that my granddad was playing harder and giving me tougher shots, and I was still winning. I really knew, of course, those times he let me win, and I loved him for it! As my skills improved, he made it tougher to win. And I treasure what he taught all of us about rejoicing when the other guy wins. Although admittedly, my cousins and I still have work to do on this!

"Granddad asked me to tell you that finding humor in today's ceremony is okay. Feel free to laugh. And feel free, too, to be sorrowful and weep. However, Granddad expected more laughter than tears in this next presentation. He even warned that if you didn't laugh, he'd be sorely disappointed."

At this, the people sitting before my grandson do laugh and he smiles at them before silently turning and unveiling a large portrait. He visibly draws himself up, so that he appears taller, and says, "Ladies and gentlemen, on behalf of his four very lucky and very proud grandchildren, I am proud to introduce my granddad—Mr. Keep Your Lights On—Tom Gunnels."

Quickly and quietly, Matt returns to his seat. The other three grandchildren stand as he rejoins them and then all four sit down together. The audience is silent, uncertain, as each ponders what Matt's introduction means. What's going to happen next?

I Celebrate My Own Life!

Danny Harb works his magic with the adjustment of a few knobs. He presses the "play" button and a voice begins to speak: "Good evening, ladies and gentlemen. Your coming tonight will mean a great deal to Frankie; to Susan and Sandra; to my grandchildren, Matt, Melissa, Lauren, and Conner; and to my sons-in-law, Ben and Lacy. And thank you, Danny, for the acoustics!"

(Danny Harb and his family are special friends of the Gunnels family. And so my voice emerges with no distortion. Everyone can hear it. Danny has me coming through loud and clear!)

"I wish you could see your faces right now, as I see them. You would hardly believe your eyes, or rather ears! Some of my tennis pals may even be thinking that this is a direct line, but let me assure you that this was indeed recorded earlier!

"Rest assured—pardon the pun—and lighten up. What I have to say will not be maudlin. I don't even know what *maudlin* means, so it can't be that! My tennis-playing buddies will remember that I owned the highest tennis toss on earth. Well, guess what, folks, my toss is the highest up here too!

"Yes, we do play tennis here, but we don't argue over the line calls. That's because no one argues with the linesman. You see our linesman not only has 20/20 vision, but he also calls them like he really sees them! With these improved line calls, I'm now winning more games up here than I ever did there. Now why would that be?

"I can just imagine what some of you might say about my speaking today. 'Ole Tom had to give his own eulogy just to make sure it's done correctly!' There may be more than a little truth to that. But of all things, this is not a eulogy. It's a thanksgiving for a life I loved living and for family and friends whom I loved living it with. It's also a plea that you will not bury with me what we have learned and shared together.

"Each one of us is charged with two responsibilities: We must keep our lights on so that we will not stumble on our journey to God, and more importantly, we must keep our light on so that those who are following us will not lose their way. Perhaps one whose light has grown dim or temporarily gone out will find a way to relight his or her lamp because our lights shine brightly. We can't be beacons if our lights don't shine.

"All of you know that at times my own lamp has grown dim. But always I have had the good sense to seek resources to relight my lamp. Many of you have been those sources. Thank you for helping me keep my lights on.

"Life presents us with many choices. and we are all responsible for our own choices. We can choose to treat ourselves as victims, or we can choose to be victors. A world of difference exists between those two choices.

"You have heard my stories about Hanover, where I was born. Hanover is a time and a place for me, just as there is a 'Hanover' that is a time and a place for you. For me, Hanover represents a place where many did not have dreams, and so they lived as victims of their circumstances. My family and I did not choose to live that way. Why? Because we knew that victims seldom reach the mountaintop, and what we wanted was the view from that mountaintop.

"I have not done all the things I wanted to do or could have done. I am still in the developmental mode for God calls us to be always developing, always seeking the best that is within us. Our Maker may not have created us all equal, but God did give each of us more talents than we are currently using.

"Sadly, too, many of us have talents that we are not making plans to use—and that's a great tragedy. I give thanks to Ralph Waldo Emerson who gave me a guidepost by saying, 'What I most need is someone or something to get me to do what I already know how to do and what I've already said I wanted to do.'

"I recognize that need in myself, and I proudly associate with people who hold me accountable for my time and my talents. To all of you who have helped me hold fast to my quest to seek a higher level, a better me, I am grateful. Make that eternally grateful! There is no greater contribution than the gift of encouragement. It's a gift that I seek to give, and it is a gift I'm always grateful to receive.

"Deciding to keep our lights on is the single most important decision we can make. It puts us in charge and takes away the feeling that we might be a victim of chance or circumstance. And I want to say to you today that if circumstance has cast a spell of doom on your life, then change that circumstance!

"Since we cannot always have what we want, we must learn to want what we have. Tragically, by its very nature, discouragement—which we all face at some time—makes us seek out others who will agree with us and verify our despair. In so doing, we perpetuate the very difficulty that is causing our problem. A wiser choice is to seek the company of those whose lights are on so that our path will be clear and we can relight our own lights.

"I had the great good fortune to spend my junior and senior years at Freeport High School, which was one of the best school systems in Texas. The teachers there took this kid from the sticks of Hanover and opened up windows to a new world that enlarged my vision and expanded my horizons.

"Miss Katharine Street, my algebra teacher and counselor, believed in me and my abilities. 'Thomas,' she once said, 'there is a grand world out there waiting for you. Go for it. There is more inside you than you realize. Let it out.'

"It was she who first got me interested in writing; then in student government. Finally, she helped me come out of my shell by encouraging me to join Little Theater. (I know, some folks may think Miss Street overdid it when she got me out of that shell!) Always Miss Street took a special pride in me, not just in high school but in all the years that followed.

"Imagine my joy when Miss Street was one of the first to greet me here. 'Thomas,' she said, 'I never doubted for a minute that you could.' Her smile was a mile wide. She was a staunch member of my balcony while she lived, after she died, and now here too. Thank you, Miss Street.

"I have been blessed with some wonderful people in my balcony, people who saw qualities in me before I was able to see them. Sue, my first wife. Frankie. My sister, Jean Dietz. My dad. Cecil F. Adam, W. W. Billips. George Pope. All of them have been mentors for me. They're all in my balcony. Every day of my life I call on the people in my balcony for continuing encouragement and renewal. Like all balcony people, they never fail me; they never flinch; they never falter. Wow! What a great crew!

"John Powell, one of Christendom's most published authors, has influenced my life positively.

Not only have his books enriched me, but I have had the pleasure of meeting him one-on-one and of corresponding with him. He always encouraged me to write a book to help others keep their lights on. Thanks, Father John.

"From one of John Powell's books—*Fully Human, Fully Alive*—came some great truths that have helped to light my way. Powell wrote 'Obnoxious behavior in myself and others (lying, bragging, temper tantrums, cheating) are cries of pain and a plea for help.' Well, in that spirit, I want to share today some of the great truths I have discovered in my quest to meet the challenges and opportunities of my days. As those truths helped me, so can they help you.

And I want to encourage you to consider these truths and to use them as guideposts on your journey.

"Initially I sought to understand other people. I learned in that pursuit, however, that before I could understand the behavior of others, I first needed to understand my own behavior. 'To thine own self, first understand' is one of my great truths. I encourage you to seek to understand yourself and then to reach out to others with understanding.

"Another great truth that has seen me through this life is that the best way to stay encouraged is to encourage others. Regularly! It is impossible to be down if you are helping someone else be up. So stay encouraged by encouraging others!

"And here's another truth I want to offer you: If you want dividends in any aspect of your life—in your homes, with your loved ones, in your places of worship, in the community, and in your professions and businesses—make an investment. You cannot earn a dividend on an investment you haven't made. So invest your life in others. Invest in being a light for them.

"Another truth that has guided my life is to play and hear my music while I live. I hope that I have played all the music within me. And I hope that you and all those in your world enjoy the music that lives in you. Live the music, the melody, the song, the talents!

"Please remember another truth that's been important to me: This life is not a dress rehearsal. It's the real thing. And the more we treat it as the real thing, the more we get done. Whatever you're going to do today, you have one shot at it. Take it!

"One of my prayers has always been that I would not die before my death. I believe that one of the great tragedies of life is to die without ever knowing—or worse, not seeking to know—the best within ourselves. I am still working on finding my best.

"This reminds me of that great prayer, 'Oh God, you know I ain't what I ought to be; and you know I ain't' what I used to be; and I'm promising I ain't what I'm gonna be.' The greatest tragedy in life is to have God-given talents and opportunities and waste them by not using them. Use your talents!

"I encourage you to choose your battles carefully. Don't fight those you cannot win. And don't fight those that aren't worth winning. Fight only when fighting is important, when the consequences of failing to fight would be obvious in the years ahead. When an issue meets that standard, then fight with courage and conviction.

"Remember, too, that praise—both of adults and children—is far more effective than criticism or punishment. Instead of spending your time defining errors and being critical, accomplish good by regularly catching people doing things right and by commending them. At least twice a week, write a brief letter of praise to someone who merits it. Practice praise. It is the most underused power on earth!

"I believe that only two kinds of people live in this world—those who turn off lights—they are the first ones to curse the darkness—and those who turn lights on. Choose to be a lamplighter all your days.

"Remember me as being in your balcony. Wherever you are, whatever you do, call on me. I'll be there. I'll encourage you to keep your lights on and to help others keep their lights on. I'll encourage you, too, to seek always the best that is within you in all aspects of your life.

"I want to say a special thanks to all of you for being in my balcony. You mean so much to me. Remember our good times, our good fun, our encouragement of each other. Thanks for helping me to keep my lights on.

"When I died, I was not through with all I could do or all I wanted to do. Still, I give thanks for the time I had. And so I encourage you to celebrate the great years we have all had together. Please, do not mourn the time we did not have. Let us all rejoice for those of us who have kept our lights on! We have been beacons for one another!"

And so I end my eulogy of myself and the ceremony continues. As you read this, you can fill in the rest: the recessional, the regaling of stories in the parish hall, the expressions of joy, the good times recalled.

BEGIN TO PLAN YOUR OWN CELEBRATION

I hope that the celebration of my life will become a source of strength for all my friends and family. I have tried to live my life in such a way that others find the strength to be their best. My celebration reveals who I have been during all the years of my journey through life.

Let my celebration catapult you into maintaining a stronger resolve to seek the magic in the moment, to be more uplifting in spirit displayed and in spirit encouraged.

Be assured that at the end of your life, your "audience" will celebrate greatly because there will be more to celebrate. Wait no more. Visualize your final celebration. Write your epitaph. Determine how others will remember you. That celebration, that epitaph, those remembrances are the map that will lead you forward.

You are on a journey, and you can make a map that will light your way. Make your map carefully, prayerfully, and thoughtfully. How do you want to be remembered? The answer to that question is the map you prepare to guide you on your journey.

Only if you consciously decide what you want as the end result of your life will you keep your lights on as you move toward that final celebration of all your life has been.

Your choice is clear—either lightness or darkness. Only in seeking the light will you find it. And you will also find focus, encouragement, and enthusiasm. These will help you keep your lights on. Then you can be a beacon for other.

To maintain your lights and keep them shining brightly, you need a map. That is, you need guidelines that show who you want to be for yourself and others. To begin to establish your guidelines, complete Worksheet 2 on page 54.

KEEP YOUR LIGHTS ON BY DOING THE FOLLOWING:

1. Decide how you want others to remember you. Remember that their "memories" are a map for your life.
2. Discover your own great truths, then record them and share them with others.
3. Keep your lights on so that you can find your own way and so that you can become a beacon for others.
4. When your lights dim, seek out those whose lights shine.
5. Remember that your choices determine the quality of your life.
6. To keep your own lights on, help others keep theirs on.
7. Say in the developmental mode throughout your whole life.
8. Understand yourself; then you can understand others.
9. Remember that you don't earn dividends on investments you haven't made. Conversely, to earn dividends in your life, invest in yourself and in others.

10. Play all the music, sing all the songs, use all the talents, seize all the opportunities God gives you.
11. Fight only those fights that are worth winning.
12. Be a lamplighter; curse, and cure, the darkness.

WORKSHEET 2
HOW OTHERS WILL REMEMBER ME

To keep your lights on, you need to perpetually audit where you are emotionally, intellectually and spiritually. You do part of this "audit" when you think about your funeral and how people there will remember you. How do you want others to remember you? What do you want to be for them and for yourself? What words do you want them to say about you at your funeral?

For this worksheet, describe how others will remember you. Their words will then become the "map" that will guide you on your journey through life. If you want to be remembered a certain way, then you must live that way.

Remember: you are not setting anything in concrete. You can change your answers whenever you like. You can change yourself.

Others Will Remember Me in This Way

Getting in Touch with Your Past

3

The People in Your Balcony

"Who are the people in your balcony?" That's the question I ask people who attend my seminars. It's also the question I asked when I recently sat across the table from a man seeking to refocus his life. (Suffering from burnout, he had experienced major job difficulties and a divorce and had come to me for help.)

My friend wasn't sure he even had a balcony, much less any balcony people. But I assured him that among my richest blessings is a well-staffed balcony and that I know who the people in it are. I can—and often do—call on them by name.

Without fail, when I call on the people in my balcony, they give me the encouragement I need. Each one has positively influenced my life in my past and that influence continues today. The process of remembering their contributions to my development energizes me, helps me refocus, encourages me, and keeps me enthused about all that challenges me each and every day.

If I am experiencing a feeling of despair or if I am feeling "down," the people in my balcony help me replace those feelings with renewed determination and zest. In short, my lights come back on. That's exactly what I want for you.

A Look Back at My Life

As you reflect on who's in your balcony, my personal journey can serve as a compass. I was born in an impoverished area of central Texas—Hanover, Milam County. The road into Hanover from Cameron (the county seat, which was located 12 miles to the west) formed a T with another road that ran south about seven miles to Gause and north for another seven miles to Milano. My father's combination country grocery-service station-blacksmith store stood about a hundred yards from that intersection.

We lived in a house across the road from our store. Homes in Hanover had no running water, no electricity, no telephone, no insulation. Our house, however, was one of the better ones because at one time—but not in my memory—it had been painted. Also, one electric light bulb of 25 watts hung in each room of our house. (Our electric lights made us the envy in our community!)

The 25-watt bulbs drew their energy from batteries charged by a Delco gasoline engine at the store. Thus, our lights were DC electric. Our radio operated on a dry-cell battery, and we didn't have electricity for running water, refrigeration, or heating. (In the winter, heat came from a fireplace in one room, a wood heater in another room. The wood-burning cook stove warmed the kitchen-dining room. Two other rooms had no heat at all.) Immediately adjacent to our home was the wash house. Next to it stood the smoke house. Close by was the outhouse, where we kept the Sears and Roebuck catalog.

My dad once observed that the dusty soil around Hanover "wouldn't grow black-eye peas." (His description made me believe that black-eyed peas would grow anywhere!) The land, however, did grow cotton, corn, and tomatoes. In addition to our country store, our family earned a living by farming five acres of tomatoes "on the halves," which meant that the landowner got half the crop. In any event, five acres of tomatoes is a lot of plants to set, water, hoe, cultivate, inspect for worms, and harvest. (And harvest and harvest!)

Next to our store stood a two-room schoolhouse where 35 students attended grades one through seven. In 1935, I was in the first grade and my older brother in the seventh. The following year, the Hanover school closed. Thereafter, a school bus took us to Milano, a consolidated school. It was somewhat larger than our Hanover school, but still so small that each year the high school would graduate only 10 to 12 seniors.

My dad's education had ended with his junior year in high school, which was still far more than the typical educational level for that time in and around Hanover. In those years, many parents desperately needed their sons and daughters to help out on the farm. They probably reasoned that no one needed a high school diploma to till the soil, slop the hogs, and harvest the crops.

When my father and mother married, he drove a team of mules for a 5000-acre farm known as the Black Farm. The owner paid both my mother and father a dollar a day and gave them housing and garden rights, which enabled them to grow most of their own foods.

From that modest income, Dad and Mom saved enough to make the down payment on a store about three miles from where they lived on the Black Farm. That store was their slice of the American dream, the ticket to providing their children with advantages—like a college education—that had not been available to them.

Dad's store served a large farming community. He extended credit that his customers usually, but not always, paid when their harvest came in. My dad and mom were strong people. Not only did they endure the hard-scrabble existence as hired hands on the large Black Farm, but they also lost their 2-year-old son to tetanus, called lockjaw by the folks in the country.

In 1937, following a long illness with a kidney infection complicated by pregnancy, my mother and the little girl she was carrying died. At that time my younger brother was four, I was seven, and an older brother had turned 14. My sister, Jean, who was 17, was about to graduate from high school and enroll in college.

Dad devised a plan that would enable all four of us to attend college. Starting with my sister, he would finance her education for two years. Then she'd get a job teaching—some school districts in Texas hired teachers after they'd attended only two years of college. Afterward, she'd fund my older brother's college for two years. My older brother would then continue the plan by sending me. My responsibility was to finance my younger brother's college career. What my younger brother was supposed to do, I don't remember, but I'm sure it was something!

My sister sent our oldest brother for two years to Sam Houston State at Huntsville, Texas. Afterward, he joined the Air Force and served in the South Pacific in World War II. As for me and my younger brother, the G.I. Bill of Rights provided us with our college funds.

World War II's defense plants attracted many of the families from our rural community. As customers moved away, my dad's business declined. So in 1944, when he was 46, Dad and my step-mom loaded my younger brother, my stepsister, and me into his 1936 Chevrolet and filled a trailer with our personal belongings. We moved to Freeport on the Gulf Coast where my father went to work for Dow Chemical.

I inherited an excellent work ethic from my dad. My first summer in Freeport, I worked as a pan cleaner at Krause's Bakery. When school started that fall, the owner promoted me to baker's helper. The next year—my senior year in high school—I became the head baker. I determined the day's run of cakes, cookies, pies, and doughnuts. Before leaving for school each morning, after four hours of work at the bakery, I made all the dough runs, including the doughnuts, which I had fried.

I'd been away from Hanover and its poverty for only a year, so that job as head baker represented a responsible position with a good income. I worked four hours before school and an hour after school each day and eight hours on Saturday—a workweek of 33 hours. I had money in the bank and could afford a nice wardrobe. In addition, I had all the pocket money I needed. I never felt disadvantaged. In fact, I felt fortunate to have such a great job. That job helped me learn to apportion my time by priorities.

So that's a little about my early life. It formed the background for my youth and adulthood. And it helped me begin to recognize the people in my balcony. Now, let me introduce you to some of them.

A Charter Member of My Balcony

It was at Freeport High School that I met one of the most important people in my balcony. The Freeport school system was one of the state's finest. Brazoria County had oil and natural gas wells, sulfur and salt mines. In addition, its seaport facilities attracted large industries. So the county's tax base supported a school system that ranked with the best anywhere. With my background in the Milam County school system, the kind of schooling provided by Brazoria County became a life-changing event.

We moved to Freeport at the end of my sophomore year at Milano High School. That first day of registration at Freeport High is still fresh in my memory. "Thomas," the counselor asked, "which math course will you be taking?"

"Well, I've had sophomore math, so I'll be taking junior math," was my matter-of-fact response.

"You don't understand, Thomas. You'll have to make some choices among the junior-level math courses."

The idea astounded me. I had more than one choice! After discussing the possibilities, the counselor, Miss Katharine Street, recommended algebra. From the beginning of my schooling in Freeport, she took a special interest in me. In those early months, I needed to spend time with her after school so that I could keep up with the rest of the class in algebra.

Miss Street must have seen me as a 15-year-old boy, right out of the sticks of Hanover, who had a strong need for guidance and direction. Perhaps all young boys have that need. Perhaps, also, she just loved the challenge I presented. In any event, I knew then as I know now, that too few of us are blessed with a Miss Street.

At 15, I was bashful, even reticent, in expressing myself. Miss Street had a prescription for that. I was to start writing—first for the school newspaper, then for our local weekly, *The Freeport Facts*. She also suggested that I become involved in our community's Little Theater.

Buoyed up by Miss Street's belief in me, I showed up for a Sunday afternoon casting call for

Let's Grow Up. Lloyd Bond, our school's drama coach, was directing, and he chose me for the part of the politician. Memorizing my lines was easy. However, my inhibitions kept me from getting into character and saying my lines with any conviction or passion. I felt like a failure.

At one of our early rehearsals, I was reciting everything stiffly, in a monotone, without inflection or feeling. I had no inner sense of my character. To keep me encouraged, Mr. Bond had the cast members go over and over a particular scene. He wanted them to help "Thomas get into the sense of his character." Never once did Mr. Bond display his frustration—although he surely must have felt it—and he never raised his voice. "Once again, Thomas. You can get it," he would say. "Once again."

Then, without warning, Mr. Bond bounded onto the stage and took the script from my hand. "Here, Thomas," he said, "Watch me. You've got to feel the way your character feels, not the way you feel. You've got to think like your character thinks, not the way you think. You've got to talk the way your character talks, not the way you talk. You've got to forget who you are and start acting like the person you're portraying."

Holding my copy of the script and reading my lines, Mr. Bond became my character. I stood mesmerized. Then he went through the scene again, taking command of my role. As he handed the script back, he placed one hand on my shoulder and said, "Thomas, you can do that; I know you can." That afternoon, following Mr. Bond's demonstration and his expressed confidence in me, I stopped being Thomas and I became the politician in *Let's Grow Up*.

I knew, of course, that only a community Little Theater, not Broadway, was presenting the play. But it had a good following. Our local newspaper critically acclaimed the portrayal by the kid less than eight months out of Hanover. For me, the most important outcome from that experience was that I learned to focus on feelings and issues that were not my own. Such learning proved invaluable to me throughout my subsequent management career.

More roles followed in other plays, which became additional stepping-stones for me. The roles got me out of my shell and started me on the road to greater self-confidence. The skills I've used on the speakers' circuit, the success I've had in conducting hundreds of training sessions for my team of agents and others all began that Sunday afternoon on the stage of the Freeport Little Theater, with Lloyd Bond, the director, showing me how to step into a world beyond myself.

That world began with a Miss Katharine Street who saw in me a spark that could be ignited. She attended each play I acted in and read each column I wrote. Often she would add, "Thomas, there's much more in you than you realize. Let it out! Let it out! Let it out!"

(Amazingly, only when I began to write this manuscript did I begin to suspect that Miss Street may have spoken to Mr. Bond on my behalf. In my heart, I do know that much of what I have accomplished in my life was given birth at Freeport High School.)

Katharine Street has played a major role in my life. Blessed with the foundation she gave me, I faced the challenges and opportunities that awaited me. As I began my road to self-discovery, I developed a central belief in continuing, perpetual improvement.

Miss Street has always been one of the most important people in my balcony. She knew that because I often told her so, in letters and in personal visits. While she was still teaching, I visited her classroom each time I returned to Freeport. She would take a desk at the back of the room and tell her students, "You're in for a treat today. Mr. Gunnels will take over the class and teach whatever he wants to teach."

I'd begin with a Miss Street trademark. Standing before the blackboard, I'd illustrate an algebraic theorem. Stepping into the Katharine Street character I'd come to know, love, and impersonate, I'd say, "If a bunch of this is equal to a bunch of that, then a bunch of that is equal to a bunch of this." As I talked, I'd draw huge marks on the blackboard, using her enthusiastic style.

Then I'd try to help the students see that Miss Street was teaching them to think logically. She taught them, as she taught me, that if I change one side of an equation, I automatically change the other. (This concept has helped me innumerable times throughout my life.)

Next, I'd ask the students, "What do you think I learned in Miss Street's classroom?" I'd immediately answer my own question by saying, "I learned that everything in math has order and certainty. I learned to think in an orderly way, to seek a logical conclusion. It's a process I continue to follow because each time I face a new opportunity, a new challenge, I learn more about something infinitely greater than algebra or math. I learn more about me."

"What do you mean, more about you?" someone would invariably ask.

"Miss Street taught me to seek truths about myself, to uncover hidden talents within me, to seek new understandings, to dream new dreams. I learned that life, like math, is an equation. If you want more in the result—the right-hand side of the equal sign—then you've got to put more into the left-hand side. It's that complex, and that simple.

"This process, once learned, does not stop in high school or college or on your first job. It applies to every dimension of your life for the rest of your life. In this classroom, you're developing techniques of learning that'll serve you wherever you go and whatever you do.

"Now hear me well: As there was more within me than I ever suspected, so there is more within you than you've ever realized. Believe me, you can let it out, let it out, let it out."

The students would clap, and Miss Street would beam. Then, as she reclaimed her class, she'd say, with obvious satisfaction, "Thomas, I can't believe I taught all that in algebra."

"Of course you did, Miss Street," I'd say. "After all, look at what you had to work with at the time."

We'd both laugh, but I doubt if any of the students understood why we thought that line was funny.

In 1988, 42 years after my graduation from high school, I received a letter from Miss Street. I share that letter with you with considerable pride and with tears of thankfulness that Katharine Street is one of the cheerleaders in my balcony.

Dear Thomas,

The doctors say that I do not have much time left. I am writing to say thanks. You wrote to me when you were stationed on Guam and each time you were promoted in the Air Force. You wrote to me when you entered SMU and when you graduated. You wrote when you and Sue were married, when each of your two daughters was born. You wrote each time you were promoted. You wrote when Sue got sick and when she died. You wrote when you and Frankie were married and when your daughters graduated from high school and college. Always you would give me more credit than I deserved. Thanks for your thoughtfulness, but thanks especially for having been one of my students in one of my classes.

Lovingly,
Katharine Street

For 42 years, Miss Street and I had stayed in touch. This letter told me how thankful she was that I had been one of her students. Her statement amazed me. I had always been grateful for her and her help and guidance, but I had never realized until then that she was thankful for me. Maybe gratitude has to go both ways, or it's not real. Maybe, also, if you're going to be a great teacher, as assuredly she was, then you need receptive students. What she was teaching, I was ready to receive. When the student is ready, the teacher will appear.

As I write this, more than eight years after her death, I can hear Miss Street saying, "Of course you can, Thomas. There's so much in you that's dying to get out. Let it out! Let it out! Let it out!"

Each day I hear her say to me, "Thomas, I have faith in you. You'll do great things. You'll make it to the top. I've always believed in you." She never defined, nor did I ask, just what making it big would mean, but the power of her encouragement still lingers—more than 50 years after my high school graduation.

OTHER MEMBERS OF MY BALCONY

Katharine Street played a pivotal and important role in my personal growth and development. But other people have also made life-enriching contributions.

My sister, Jean Dietz, is nine years my senior. Following the death of our mother in 1937, when I was approaching eight and Jean was 17 and getting ready for college, her care for me went far beyond that of a sibling. She had a powerful, positive impact on my growth and development.

After graduating from Freeport High School, I joined the Air Force. When I finished my three-year stint, my sister urged me to use the G.I. Bill of Rights to attend Southern Methodist University in Dallas.

I thought SMU was a rich kid's school, and Hanover was such a recent part of my history that I wasn't able to picture myself attending such an affluent university. Nevertheless, Jean encouraged me to go there. Then she invited me to live with her and her family of three small children in their one-bathroom home while I attended SMU.

I accepted her invitation and lived with my sister and her family during my first two years of college. Her belief in me become part of my personal success. She is one of my long-term staunch boosters, a valued member of my balcony club.

My father is another member of my balcony. T. P., as most people called him, had high expectations for my future. He believed in me. From his humble perspectives, my SMU degree looked particularly impressive. He thought that in no time I would be heading up a major corporation! When I was 25 years old, the company for which I worked appointed me regional personnel manager. I may have been surprised, but my father wasn't!

Dad celebrated both that promotion and the next, which occurred when I was 29. That time, the company made me its first director of agency training. That same year, I became a manager of agents. Frankly, I can't imagine not working hard, not striving mightily to do my best. Why? Because my father, who worked so hard all his life, believed in me. He died in 1977, but not before he had rejoiced many times at what I had accomplished.

Another balcony member is Sue, my first wife. She married me between my sophomore and junior years at SMU and helped shape my early dreams. Sue could always find a rainbow in the darkest clouds. No mountain was too high for us to climb. She believed in our having a purpose—what we now call a mission—and holding fast to our resolve. Before and during her terminal illness, she often expressed how much faith she had in me, how proud she was to be my wife. She was absolutely certain that I would "make it big."

While she lived through the last months of her life, Sue often said to me, "Don't allow my illness or my death to keep you from doing what you know you can do. I won't live to see it happen, but I'll be there, never doubting, always believing in you. When the acclaim starts coming in, remember that I predicted it. If you listen carefully, you'll hear my applause." Then she'd hold my hand tightly and say, "Tom, we've been a great team, and we always will be."

Sue is a fixture in my balcony. She's probably saying right now, "See! I told you so! You're doing it!"

Frankie, whom I married five years after Sue's death helped me improve my vision of myself. In doing that, she also helped to improve my vision of a world I was just beginning to know.

For these past 27 years, our life has been an upward spiral. Frankie has always loved me for who I am today. But she has also loved the person I want to become. She has been my sounding board and friend. She helps me discover what I think. She is the person to whom I turn in all of life's disappointments.

Frankie and I have shared the joy of exploring the world on special award trips earned in my work.

Together, we have shared the satisfaction of rearing Susan and Sandra and seeing them earn their college degrees and marry wonderful men. When grandchildren came, Frankie found her grandmother's role a delight. She leads the cheering in my balcony. In fact, if any of my balcony members aren't cheering, she invites them to pay closer attention!

Another person in my balcony is Cecil F. Adam, the vice president who selected me to become his regional personnel manager despite the fact that other people in the company were older and had more experience than I did. Mr. Adam was a persistent booster and a good friend of mine right up to his death in 1995.

Mr. Adam has the distinction of having given me the worst dressing down I've ever received, made all the more painful because I deserved it. After spending a couple of hours detailing my errant behavior, he asked me to join him for lunch. I thought he was going to continue to rake me over the coals during our meal. The fact is that he acted as if nothing had happened. He never again brought up the subject. At his retirement dinner, I shared this story with the audience and concluded my tribute by saying, "Mr. Adam had the ability to step on your toes without messing up your shoeshine."

Cecil Adam always endorsed and applauded my advancements. Generously, he and Ruth, his wife, insisted on paying for Sue's night nurse the last few months of her life. You bet, Cecil F. Adam is in my balcony, still affirming and encouraging me to seek my best. "I never doubted for a minute what you could and would do," he's saying even now. (He's embarrassed, though, that I told you about his paying for the night nurse.)

W. W. Billips, when State Farm reorganized in 1958, became our regional vice president. He had a crucial role in my career development past the personnel manager's position. Generous, always mindful of his ability to influence others, an outstanding speaker, sincere, thoughtful, a natural-born encourager, he led by his own personal example. "Tom," he'd say, "I want you to see all the abilities you have as I see them. There's more within you than you realize."

I wanted to see what Mr. Billips could see, and so I kept striving. In increasing measures, he became my mentor; I sought to emulate him in all dimensions of my personal and professional life. In my work with the men and women on my team, I sought to behave as I believed Mr. Billips would in the same circumstance. As I worked with my team members, I applied Mr. Billips' technique of describing the positive qualities I could see in each of them. Without a Mr. Billips in my life and in my balcony, I would be far less than I am today in all facets of my life.

Another member of my balcony is George Pope, only a few years my senior. He was particularly insightful in helping me eliminate some of my negative habits. For instance, when I first knew him, I was in the habit of using self-deprecating humor that put me in an unfavorable light.

Following George's advice, I redirected the thrust of my humor.

For the four and one-half years that Sue was sick, George was my boss. I will always be grateful for his thoughtfulness and support during that long, difficult period. After Sue's death, he drove 200 miles to arrive early the following morning so he could lend support. He had an inner strength that I have sought to emulate. Count George Pope in my balcony, encouraging me even now in my second career.

Others sit in my balcony, cheering for me. Each one owns a rich part of my history. Every member of my balcony club is saying, "Come on, Tom, you can do it. Stay with it. Let those lights inside you out! Let them out! Your best is still ahead."

YOUR BALCONY

Now, who's in your balcony? I've shared these stories about some people who have greatly touched my life so as to help you remember those who have similarly helped you. Who are people from your past who have so richly touched your life that without them you could not be where you are or who you are today?

Think about those people who believed in you; who opened new windows of understanding; who encouraged you to seek something better in yourself; who helped you set a new, higher standard of study or job performance. These are your balcony people. Naming them is the first step to get in touch with your past.

But why is the past important? Because it provides the foundation for your journey as you begin to practice the art of keeping your lights on. Admittedly, you also have people in your basement. They're the naysayers, the harbingers of failure, the critics, the ones who erected barriers to personal growth and achievement within you.

Those voices in your basement often resonate so loudly that they drown out your good intentions. That's another reason to identify and know your balcony people. They help you close your ears and mind and heart to the negatives voices. They help you say, "Be quiet down there! I've got things to do."

Getting to know your balcony people is the first step on your journey. Identifying them will be an exciting and rewarding exercise as you discover the art of keeping your lights on. As you move through this first step, you begin to unfold the depth and dimensions of yourself—the person, the dreamer, the one who can do more and be more by unleashing the lights within.

You are about to enlarge your horizon. You have far more ability than you are presently able to perceive. Today, you begin to change your erroneous perception of yourself; you begin to perceive the real you in all your God-given wonder.

Right now, you may hunger for something more in every facet of your life. You can begin to fill this hunger by identifying your balcony people who have helped you develop a positive self-attitude.

The process I am now suggesting will help you maintain this healthy, upbeat, positive attitude more consistently. As one of my seminar participants asserted, "Keeping your lights on is the next step beyond the positive attitude hype."

So who are your balcony people? Consider these sources: parents, spouses, siblings, relatives, teachers, bosses, fellow workers, friends, pastors, mentors. Whatever their relationship to you, your balcony people opened for you new windows of understanding and opportunity. They affirmed your strengths. They believed in you so strongly that you took new paths. Because of them, you have a better appreciation of yourself, your talents, your abilities, your resolve.

In reality, your balcony people have given you your foundation. At the time you knew them or at the time they said something monumentally important to you about yourself or about life, you may not have realized the impact they would have on your life. But today, as you reflect on them, you become aware that their gifts to you are beyond measure.

One or more of your balcony people could have touched your life early in your childhood or perhaps as recently as last month. Start today by considering all the people who have been "encouragers" and "enthusers" at crucial times in your life.

The 5-Step Process That Helps You Begin to Keep Your Lights On

<u>Step 1:</u> Using Worksheet 3 on page 91, list your balcony people by name. That way, you can call them by name when you seek their continuing

inspiration and encouragement, even when they are not present to you.

Step 2: After listing your balcony people by name, write the qualities you most admire about each one of them. List what they did for you, what they helped you realize, how they touched your life and your beliefs, and how they continue to do so. To help you get started, let me share the descriptions I've written for some of the people in my balcony:

- Katharine Street saw qualities in me before I could see them. She enlarged my vision and opened new windows of understanding that promoted a life of self-discovery. She demonstrated the power of praise and positive expectations. She also showed me the power of writing letters to encourage and support others in their journey. She helped prepare me to meet my own challenges and opportunities.

- Sue was willing to grow and learn with me. She was careful to put me in the most favorable light, and she had great faith in me as a husband, father, and professional. She encouraged and shared my dreams and my ambitions, always demonstrating the power of unconditional love. She took the unbearable—her illness—and made it a gift.

  Sue loved being a parent and demonstrated this by preparing our young daughters for her death and for my second marriage. She could face disappointment and bounce back quicker than anyone I've ever known. She knew how to keep her lights on however difficult the circumstances.

- My dad had great expectations about what I could and would do. He had faith in me and in my abilities. He always believed I would do the right thing. When Sue died, I knew how to go on because I had seen my father go on after my mother's death. His example greatly helped me.

- Frankie has introduced me to new horizons. In my community work, she has rescued me when I got in over my head. She teaches me about the finer things in life and always wants the best for me. She demonstrates the power of not settling for one's second best. Well read, well versed, she is aware of the visual part of this world. She expresses her belief in my abilities often.

- Cecil F. Adam taught me the importance of being critical without being demeaning. He taught me to be uplifting, especially when I needed to offer criticisms and suggestions to those who worked for or with me. He demonstrated the power of fairness coupled with toughness. He always had great faith in me, and I have always wanted to affirm his belief.

- W. W. Billips was kind and gentle, but firm, in his expectations of results. He insisted that all of us who worked for him go the extra mile. He taught me that all of us wear blinders that keep us from seeing our true abilities. He demonstrated for me that the greatest gift each of us have is helping others see themselves in a positive light. His living trademark is to be consistent and persistent.
- George Pope is methodical and knows where he stands. Taking the easy road is not his inclination unless it is the preferred choice. He is always willing to listen and make adjustments according to new information. He consistently demonstrates the power of knowing one's strengths and builds on them with the power of conviction.

I hope my list of the qualities of some members of my balcony helps you complete your list. Now write those qualities next to each person you placed in your balcony.

Step 3: Next, get in touch with each person in your balcony. Write a letter to each one, including those to whom you will be unable to mail the letter. (The message is not just for them. It's for you too!) Make no exception. Let each one know how grateful you are that he or she is in your balcony. I wrote to Miss Street many times during the 42 years between my high school graduation and her death. Here's the letter I would write today:

Dear Miss Street,

Can you believe it? It's been more than 50 years since I was in your class at FHS! As I've said before, and I'll say again, I'm richly blessed for having been a student in your classes. I am the beneficiary of your teaching and your enthusiasm for me and for my future. You have richly impacted my success along every step of the way.

Thanks for believing in me. I know I'm not yet where I want to be or should be or will be. But this much I know: Whatever I do will be the result of the foundation learned in your classroom at FHS. You are in my balcony, and I call on you every day. You never fail me.

Thanks always.
Thomas

Here are four letters about balcony members. (Members of my seminars sent me these letters after they wrote their balcony letters.) The first comes from a father and a son who piloted their own planes to hear my KYLO presentation in Anchorage. Afterward, the son wrote his father the following letter to thank him for being in his balcony:

Dear Dad,

You constantly say how proud you are of me. I am also very proud and honored by you. You are all and more than anyone could ever want or need as a father and friend. I love you. Applying the lessons you taught will reduce your odds of getting lost. Work hard, be patient, learn and persevere, and you will get results. Stay on course. We would be lost without you.

Love,
Your son, Ed

From the Tri-Cities, I received the following letter from someone who attended my seminary and wrote to a teacher:

My first letter went to my high school vocational ed teacher. He called a couple of days later, crying, telling me how much he appreciated being in my balcony. He died four days later—with my letter in his coat pocket. His widow then called and asked if I would deliver the eulogy at his funeral. When I protested that I did not know how to do that, she said simply, "Just read the letter you wrote to him."

Earl Jarnigan
Insurance management
Newport, Tenn.

My presentation to the world's largest gathering of Episcopal laymen produced this letter to me:

I wrote to a fellow high school student whom I had not seen in 20 years. In high school, he had always carried a Bible and frequently engaged us in religious discussions. I had such respect that I did not tell off-color stories in his presence. My letter told him about my Christian conversion recently which reminded me of the powerful, positive model he had provided in high school. He wrote back, "Your letter could not have been more timely. I am going through some difficult times and have been wondering if God cared about my problems or if he were listening to my prayers. Through your letter, I feel God is speaking to me, does care. You say the seed I planted with you brought you to the Lord. Well, your faith—expressed in your letter—has reawakened mine. God works in strange, mysterious and wonderful ways."

Jim Dillon
Murfreesboro, Tenn.

Finally, here's a letter I received from Bob Butler, president of the chamber of commerce in Mount Sterling, Ky.

Dear Tom,

I wrote to one of my balcony people, the housemother at my college fraternity. She's in her 80s now. I let her know the power of her influence on me—when I was in college and still even today. She called me promptly to tell me how thrilled she was to hear that she had positively influenced me. My business, Tom, goes exceptionally well because I am keeping my lights on. Every day that I turn on someone's lights my own lights shine brighter.

As you can see, writing these letters is important—for you and for the person to whom you write. In these letters, you express your gratitude for what each person in your balcony has done in your life. You won't be able to mail some of the letters for the people will have died. But they are still rooting for you. Other, those still alive, will receive your letters and take hope and encouragement from them.

Step 4: Write a letter to you from each person in your balcony. That's right—write the letter to yourself, but compose the letter as you believe each balcony person would write it today. Make the assumption that each one knows where you are in your progress and that he or she knows, as you do, that you're not through growing. What would each balcony member say to you today? Write their words down as their letter to you.

To illustrate Step 4, let me share with you the letters I think some of my balcony cheerleaders would write to me. Here's what Katharine Street would write today:

> Dear Thomas,
>
> I'm very proud of all you have done, but what I'm most proud of is that you're not done with your doing! You're still looking for new mountains to climb. As proud as I am of your achievements, I believe that what lies ahead of you will be even bigger. Keep me posted as you reach each one of your new plateaus, but remember—they *are* plateaus, not your final resting place. Yes, there is more inside you to let out. Let it out, Thomas! Let it out!
>
> Lovingly,
> Katharine Street

My father, T. P. Gunnels, would write the following:

Dear Son,

I can't wait until you finish the book. I just know that it will make the best-seller list in short order. You'll be on all the TV talk shows telling the world about *Keep Your Lights On.* I told the folks down at the bookstore to order your book. They said they would just as soon as it comes off the press. You've got a powerhouse of a message. Hang in there, son, as you always have, hang in there. Keep on keeping on. Tell the world your *Keep Your Lights On* story. I'm so excited about what's ahead.

Love,
Dad

Sue, my first wife, would write:

Dear Tom,

You've been wondering if you've made it as big as I thought you would. Making it big means reaching beyond where you are and going for that next level. Each new step along the way gives you another view of what you can yet become. Making it big is not a specific time and place. Making it big means you're still striving, still seeking the best that is within you. You continue to make it big by still seeking personal improvement. I always knew you'd be like that.

Love,
Sue

Cecil F. Adam, the vice president who chose me as his personnel manager, would write:

Dear Tom,

What a fabulous first career you had! Ruth and I are not the least bit surprised. We expected it all along. Your second career will be even more challenging and rewarding. Keep working at it with the same innovation and effort you displayed in your first career. Thanks for always making my faith in you so well founded. Your best is yet to be.

Love,
Cec and Ruth

Frankie, my wife, agrees that this is her kind of letter to me:

Dear Honey,

Trust your convictions, your beliefs, your dreams. Much has been accomplished and more lies ahead. Listen to the voice inside you that confirms there is more you want to do and will do. I'm very proud of what you have done, but I am prouder still that there is more that you want to do, can do, and will do. Hold on to your dream. I'm proud to be part of your dreaming. Go for it all. Remember that I'm proud that you're still dreaming, still wanting to do more. You're a seeker, a quality I greatly admire. Persist. Persist. Persist.

Love,
Frankie

You know your balcony people well, and each one of them knows you. In your heart, you know what kind of advice and encouragement they would say to you in a letter they would write today. Write the letter to you as they would write it. The letter will illustrate how well you know those who have so richly influenced you.

These letters demonstrate that you are still in touch with the power of their influence and with their faith in you. The letters also show that you are still listening to them. To help you begin, review my letters as a way to be in touch with the kind of letter you will be writing.

Step 5: Save the letters from your balcony members. Why? Because at some future time you may need to remember their caring for you. Through these letters, they will bless you again and again.

AN AFTERWORD

The five-step process you just completed can be a major learning event for you. You now know not only the kind of person you want to be, but also the kind of person you have been prepared to become. The people in your balcony show you the way to a better you. They are God's gift to you.

When you acknowledge the balcony people who have helped to make you who or what you are today, you realize that you are not self-made; you have not walked alone. To think otherwise is to deceive yourself.

To avoid such self-deception learn the truths about yourself. These truths will help you become focused, encouraged, and enthused. As a result, you will achieve a higher level of personal fulfillment. Why does this happen? Because you realize your potential in your personal and your professional life. The first truth you must learn is the truth of your balcony people.

Letter from "Keep Your Lights On" Seminar

Dear Tom,

Prior to hearing you speak, I never had thought deeply about the few special people who had clearly made a positive significant difference in my life; I had never tried to use my mind's eye to literally see them "in my balcony"; I had never made a planned conscientious attempt to let them know of my appreciation for them before it was too late. After hearing you speak, I took care of that matter, I believe without excepting anyone still living, and some I have told more than once. At this time I will share one of these experiences:

I am 51 years old and the 12th of 14 children from eastern Kentucky, specifically Perry County in Appalachia. My dad, who died at the age of 91 in 1994, had a third-grade education; my mother, who died at the age of 89 a few days ago, completed the eighth grade.

In 1953, when I was six years old, we arrived in Montgomery County, which is on the edge of what is known as central Kentucky. My dad was financially broke, there were eight children at home, and his employment background centered entirely around coal. Since there were no coal mines in central Kentucky, Dad got a job as a janitor in the school system. Thereafter, I and most of my brothers and sisters helped sweep and clean the buildings.

Though we were very poor financially, my dad and mom always exhibited enormous love and encouragement to us. My mom often told me, from the time I was five years old until I graduated from college, that someday I was going to do something special. I don't know what my mom was talking about, and I'm not sure she knew for sure, but I think my mom did something special by encouraging me to get an associate degree, then a bachelor's degree, then a master's, then a Rank I in administration (30 hours beyond the master's degree), and finally, a doctorate in educational administration which helped me to become the superintendent of schools in the district where I once swept the floors.

After hearing you speak in 1996, I made a point to convey my appreciation to my mother for what she had done for me. Fortunately for me, on the day of her death, I visited her at the hospital from 9 to 9:30 a.m., a time when I rarely visited as I normally would visit after work in the evenings or on Sunday afternoons.

Before I left that morning, I kissed my mother and told her how much I loved her. I came to my office and was diligently at work when nurse Sharon Follett called and said mom had just died.

As far as I know, my becoming superintendent of schools in Montgomery County was that something special that she expected me to accomplish as she never hesitated to tell almost everyone with whom she spoke what her son did. However, to me that something special was having the opportunity to visit with my mother that morning before she died and to thank her for "being in my balcony."

Richard Hughes,
Superintendent of
Montgomery County Schools
Mount Sterling, Ky.

KEEP YOUR LIGHTS ON BY DOING THE FOLLOWING:

1. Identify each person in your balcony.
2. List by each person the qualities you most admire in that person.
3. Write a personal letter to each person in your balcony, including those whom you will not be able to send your letter.
4. Write yourself a letter from each of the people in your balcony.
5. Save the letters you wrote to yourself.
6. Combine all the qualities on your list into one list so that you will understand the kind of person you want to be and have been prepared to become.
7. Resist taking short cuts in this 5-step process of finding your balcony people. Remember that persistency and consistency win every time.
8. Use this exercise as a way of getting in touch with your past. Remember that your past is the foundation for learning to keep your lights on.

WORKSHEET 3
THE FIVE-STEP PROCESS THAT HELPS ME GET IN TOUCH WITH MY PAST

Steps 1 and 2

List the names of the people in your balcony. Underneath each name, list the quality or qualities you admire about him or her.

Step 3

Write a letter to each balcony person, living or dead. Keep a copy of each letter. Send each letter that can be mailed.

Steps 4 and 5

Write a letter to you *from* each balcony person. In your letter, reflect that person's style of advice and commendation about the progress you are making to achieve your personal and career goals. Keep these letters for your future reference.

4

Your Child Within

In my seminars, I use a favorite exercise to help the participants find the child inside themselves and discover how that child influences them today. At first, many of them are reluctant to admit that they have an inner child or that this child can influence them today. But all learn, as you will, that the child within each of us influences what we do and say today and how we view the world.

There is a child inside each of us. In this chapter, examine how the child in you affects your life today. The ultimate question posed by this chapter is "How does the child inside you control your behavior today?"

Let's begin with an exercise I've developed to help you answer that question.

A FOUR-STEP EXERCISE FOR GETTING IN TOUCH WITH YOUR UNMET CHILDHOOD WANTS

You can never get enough of what you did not have when you were eight to 10 years old. For the rest of your life, you compensate—unconsciously—for what you lacked as a child. Read those two sentences again, for their truth has profound importance in keeping your lights on. This age span is important for a couple of reasons:

Our memories are usually clear and recallable for that time in our lives.

Wants and desires are well-formulated by then. That makes them trustworthy for recollection.

Now, let's find out what you wanted, but didn't get, when you were eight to 10 years old. To do this, let's follow a four-step exercise.

Step 1: Using Worksheet 4 on pages 110–111, answer, as completely and specifically as you can, the following question: What was your childhood like when you were eight to 10 years old?

To help you get into the spirit of Step 1, I'd like to share with you something about my life.

When I was approaching eight years of age, I lost my mother following her long illness. It's true that I had an older sister who cared greatly for me. It's also true that my father married again 18 months after my mother's death. Nevertheless, this loss was monumental for me because my mother was gone and because a well-intentioned adult stupidly suggested that "God must have needed another angel, and that's why He called your mother."

That statement filled me with anger toward God. He could create the universe. Couldn't he see that I needed my mother? Wasn't my need greater than his for another angel? Thus, at eight, I not only lost my mom, I also lost God.

What happened to you when you were eight to 10 years old? Where did you live—in the city or in a rural setting? How many brothers and sisters were at home then? What did your home look like? What kind of work did your father do? Was your mother employed outside the home? Did you move a lot? Were you sickly? Were your creature comforts adequate? Who were your best friends? What were your favorite activities? Did you do well in school?

Think about yourself at eight to 10 years old. Who were you then? Write your answer under Step 1 of Worksheet 4.

Step 2: Next, write your answer to the following question: What do you remember wanting, but not getting, when you were eight to 10 years old?

Once again, I'll share something about myself to help you begin to answer this question.

What I most wanted when I was eight was my mom. I also wanted to be able to trust God again. Beyond that, I wanted a birthday party and a present. As a child, I'd never had any kind of birthday celebration. Nor had anyone ever given me a gift.

When I was eight, I daydreamed about a wonderful party with friends and relatives gathered around me. They were all smiling and loving me. I imagined myself opening each beautifully wrapped package, cutting the ribbon, exclaiming, "Oh, you shouldn't have." But I knew that I'd have added under my breath, "But I'm sure glad you did."

What would be in those beautiful packages? A bicycle, a watch, and shiny shoes.

In Hanover, we received in the mail the Sears and Roebuck catalog at least twice each year. Those huge books listed all kinds of toys, clothes, jewelry, and general merchandise. Each time the catalog came, I checked three sections. First I turned to the toys. Out of all the toys pictured in the catalog, all I wanted was a bicycle. But not just any bicycle. I wanted one of those Schwinn bikes with a horn, fancy fenders, and an electric light.

In my imagination, I could see myself riding like the wind down a dusty hill, laughing, grinning from ear to ear, having the time of my life! I dreamed of the wonder of this, but I never had that bike, except in my mind.

Next, I checked the catalog for watches. I imagined how glorious owning one of those seven-jewel $7.95 watches would be. I visualized walking around with my arm extended so I could see that watch and show it off to others. I'd be so happy to have one of those golden watches! But a watch never adorned my wrist until I was 15.

Finally, I looked at the catalog pictures of wonderfully polished shoes. I had always had shoes to cover my feet, but I wanted shoes that shined, that I could see my image in when I leaned over and looked down. Had I owned shiny shoes, I would have walked bent over so I could admire their luster!

After looking at the catalog pictures of those beautiful shoes, I'd walk around our house and yard, strutting as if I owned just such a pair. But the shiny shoes I so much wanted did not come until much later.

Now, what did you want, but not get, as a child? What was missing in my life as a youngster? On Step 2 of Worksheet 4, list all the things you remember passionately wanting. Do you remember wanting, but not getting, a particular toy, certain kinds of clothing, some kind of jewelry? Did you want a better relationship with a parent or a brother or a sister? Did you want better health care?

Do you remember wanting, but not getting, more acceptance from one or more members of your family or from your classmates? Did you want and not get economic security? Peace? Good grades? A position on the ball team? A younger brother or sister? Fewer fights in the family? On Worksheet 4, write down a list of all you wanted, but never got, when you were young.

Step 3: Finally, select three items from your list of "wants" when you were eight to ten years old. Place these items at the top of your "most wanted" list for when you were young.

Here are the top three things I wanted and never got when I was in the eight-to-10-year-old bracket:

- A mother.
  All my friends had moms, and I was mad at God for putting his need for another angel ahead of my need for a mom.
- A birthday party with gifts wrapped in beautiful paper. Those gifts would mean that I was really loved.
- A bicycle, a watch, and shiny shoes.
  I passionately wanted all three.

What were your top "wants" when you were eight to ten years old? What did you want passionately and what did you not get? Write your wants under Step 3 on the worksheet.

Later in this chapter, you'll complete Step 4 of the worksheet. But first, I want to share with you how these unmet wants can affect your life today.

HOW MY UNMET WANTS AFFECT ME TODAY

All the major childhood wants that weren't satisfied when I was young have influenced my life. Remember my passion to own a bicycle, a watch, and those shiny shoes when I was a child? Would you care to guess what kind of shoes I have in my wardrobe today? Shiny shoes! And how many pairs? Twelve! Even so, I still check out the shoes in every department store I enter and in every clothing catalog that comes to our home.

What about that watch I so desperately wanted? Do you think I have a nice gold watch today?

Maybe several watches? How about six? Yet I still check out the watches in displays and magazines, even though I concede that I have enough now. That doesn't mean, however, that I won't get another watch, in an unguarded moment!

That leaves my intense desire for a Schwinn bicycle. Do you think I have one of those in my garage today? One with fancy tires, lights, perhaps a horn or a bell? You may miss this one because, in truth, I still don't own a bike and never have. But I have owned several bicycle substitutes, and they have all the bells and whistles I so much wanted as a child. My bicycle substitutes? They're called Cadillac, Lincoln, Lexus, Mercedes.

What about the missing birthday party, the cake, the presents? How does that longing impact my life today? Based on what you've learned thus far, make a guess about how I feel about birthdays— anyone's birthday. Do I remember them? Celebrate them? Send cards, letters, presents? Do you think I make a big deal about birthdays? Do you think that each of my children and my grandchildren received a bicycle and a watch and shiny shoes early in their lives? If you answered yes to all those questions, then you've begun to see how my past influences my present.

The fact is, I want birthday celebrations for everyone, so for more than 30 years of my career as an agency manager, I gave each of the agents with whom I worked a birthday party each year. I'd arrive at the office with a decorated cake, a birthday banner, candles, and the needed plates and forks. The agent's office staff would arrange the coffee or cold beverages. I'd have a camera and snap all the happy scenes and the participants in the celebrations. A couple of days later, I'd mail the developed pictures to the agent with a penned note, "Happy Birthday all over again."

What about my not having a mom and my anger at God? Wanting a mom has strongly influenced my life. I honor mothers. I honored my stepmother; I honor my wife; I honor the mothers of my grandchildren. The ache in my heart for my missing mom is monumental, beyond all normal understanding. It probably explains why I have always tried to nurture others.

What about my anger with God? My struggle with this has been long and arduous. My anger dissipated only in my second year in the Air Force. I was stationed on Guam. There, as I had in high school, I made friends with people who could stretch me intellectually and spiritually. Gradually, they helped me understand that what really angered me was a thoughtless comment made by someone who meant well but who did not understand the damage such a statement about God and angels and my mother could cause.

One night, all alone, I went outside my barracks at Tumon Bay. Gazing at the full moon, I got down on my knees, and God and I came to an understanding. I prayed for God to forgive me for all those years I had been blaming him. At that moment, I felt great relief as I released years of accumulated anger. Today I give thanks to all those wonderful people who helped me reach that understanding.

All these major childhood wants that were not satisfied when I was a child have influenced my life. They had an impact on me when I was young. But they also affect me now, many, many years later. I acknowledge their collective impact on me.

How Your Unmet Wants Affect You

As I have done, you can examine how your major unmet childhood desires affect you today. You can examine how your child, your childhood, is still with you.

To find out how your childhood still influences you, review the list you made in Step 2 and Step 3 on Worksheet 4. Then consider, for Step 4, the behavioral characteristics that you demonstrate today that you can attribute to those unfulfilled wants of your childhood. What do you do today that represents who you were as a child and what needs you had then that were not met?

Spend time thinking about that child and those wants. Watch yourself and your actions in the days and weeks ahead. Return to Step 4 of Worksheet 4 each time you discover something new about how the past influences your present. Ask yourself again and again, "Does this behavior reflect any lack in my childhood?"

Why do I want you to do this? Because the child in you still influences your actions, still makes you react to certain stimuli. Only when you understand and accept this can you determine who you now want to be. Your past can help or hinder you. If you want to use it as a stepping-stone to your growth, you must understand who you were and what you wanted as a child.

So look at your behavior today and consider how it flows out of your past. Then consider how much you want your past to influence your present. Remember, you can choose to change. Acknowledging your past gives you mastery over your present.

WHO'S IN CONTROL?

The question is no longer whether there's a child in you. Most of us have probably accepted that. Now we must ask ourselves, "How much is that child in control?" We cannot eliminate the influence of our child within, nor should we try. But we can understand this child and this child's wants. When we understand, we are able to keep the influence of the child within us in perspective. At the very least, we need not visit upon the succeeding generations our childhood feelings of anger and inadequacy.

We must also avoid using our past as a crutch to prevent us from making real, meaningful changes in the way we view the world. On the contrary, we must examine ourselves and seek a better understanding. In the final analysis, we are—each one of us—responsible for who we are, where we are, and where we are going. We are not victims of our past. To view ourselves as victims is to relinquish control of our destinies.

None of us changes until and unless we become accountable for what happens now. We do not ask victims to make a change in their outlook. We do not demand that they understand the child within. But we are not victims. We are doers; we are ones who can triumph. When we accept that we are individually responsible for who and what we are, where we are now, and where we are going, we begin to change. Great things happen when we take charge of our own destinies.

Getting to know the child inside makes us stronger, more resilient, more resourceful. Getting to know that child and its wants can also make us more sensitive to others.

THE UNMET WANTS OF OTHERS

Understanding your own wants as a child and how they affect you helps you take control of your life. This understanding can also help you become more tolerant and more loving toward others. Consider some of the behavioral characteristics of those you love—your spouse, your children, your parents, your friends, perhaps some of the people with whom you work. Based on the behaviors you have seen them demonstrate, what are some of the likely childhood sources that may account for what you see?

Once again, you may be asking, "Why would I want to do this?" The reason is simple: the insights you gain will enrich your ability to relate to other people, to help them, to understand them, to be tolerant of them, to like and love them, to wish the best for them.

As an aid to this kind of study, I'm going to list what other people have wanted, but did not have, when they were eight to 10 years old. Look over the list and think about the kinds of behaviors these people might exhibit today as a result of their passionate childhood desires that were unfilled.

- A positive, caring relationship with a father or mother.

  If a parent died or abandoned the family or if a parent was disabled or dysfunctional because of alcohol or drugs how would that affect a person today? Consider how the absence of good role modeling, of nurturing not demonstrated and received, of anger suppressed, of the lack of suitable authority figures impinges on relationships with supervisors, fellow works, and a spouse.

- Good health so that the child could play and have fun with other children.

  Consider how a serious illness or injury could make a child feel unattractive or unaccepted. Think about how poor self-esteem, a pronounced feeling of not being accepted, or perhaps feeling unattractive could make a person act. How would those feelings affect his or her happiness curve in the future?

- Food.

  Think about going to bed hungry. Could the adult who was hungry as a child ever get enough food? Perhaps that person overeats today or eats the wrong kinds of food. What about one's worry about tomorrow's food even when there is more than enough in the pantry? Could hunger for food lead to hunger for others things? To hoarding? To stinginess?

- A home that provides warmth and comfort.

  Would a person who had no home as a child feel secure as an adult? How much would that child worry about security and money? Would that person envy others? Would that person not want to leave home to visit with others?

- Adequate clothing as compared to others in the community. Would such a person feel unusually self-conscious about his or her appearance, to the point of an obsession? Also, many who felt deprived in this area also tend to insist on wearing clothes until they are 'worn-out' before discarding. My personal fixation about shiny shoes likely derives from feelings dating from that time of my life.

- Reasonable medical or dental care.

  Would the person who didn't get medical help as a child worry excessively about most aches and pains and become, possibly, a hypochondriac? Would that person be overly protective toward his or her offspring?

- A family that has been torn apart by divorce.

  Think about the abandonment that children of divorce feel. Consider how they feel that they have done something wrong and that their parents no longer love them. How might those childhood feelings affect their adult behavior?

- Safety from being abused either physically, sexually, or verbally.

  Studies show that there is a cycle to abuse, that one who is abused as a child, abuses the next generation.

- Acceptance or affirmation at home.

  How would being rejected as a child affect a person's lifelong self-esteem? Would that person be critical of others? Would that person be more or less likely to affirm and accept his or her own children?

These wants color the world of the child. That child grows into an adult with childhood still inside. As with many people who grew up during the Great Depression, the economic insecurity of that time has affected my entire life.

My parents had a difficult time during the Depression. The child in me experienced their insecurity, and even today that lack of security causes me to react in certain ways. How much of that childhood desire for security contributed to a work experience of more than 41 years with one company? The fear of losing a continuous adequate income may have kept me working for the same company for that long span of time.

The lesson for us to learn with regard to others is that we must avoid judging them. If we know anything about their childhood, we must consider how that childhood could affect them today. So we do not judge. That does not mean that we simply accept unacceptable behavior. We understand it and we stand ready to help others change—if they choose to change.

My reason for including this section on others in this chapter is because I want you to realize how important understanding yourself is. When you understand yourself, you are able to understand others. When you begin to understand others and why they act as they do, you are better able to help them, be tolerant of them, and like them.

A Final Word

This chapter helps you get in touch with the child within you and discover what that child wanted and needed and longed for in the past and how that past influences today. Understanding that child of yesterday will help you understand the you of today. What we have and what we do not have as children not only touches us in our youth but in all the years that follow.

Why is learning about this important? Because when you are able to see and understand that some of your actions today are based on events from your childhood, you gain greater mastery of yourself and your life.

We've come to the end of this chapter. I hope you can now accept the child within yourself. I hope you are grateful for all that child has given you. And I hope you realize how the wants of that child have influenced the patterns of your life.

Do you want to change any of those patterns? You can. You can become focused, encouraged, and enthused about your life and your journey. You can put your lights on and keep them lit! As this book continues, I'll show you ways to do that.

But be assured that you have already begun to keep your lights on. So thank yourself for what you have done thus far and resolve to allow yourself to do even more as you strive to become a fully realized human being!

Letter from "Keep Your Lights On" Seminar

I work with little kids. Loving them and letting them love you is important. A lot of people miss out when they don't share their love. Thanks for reminding me to share my lights.

Marvin Fowler
Active in Mothers Against
Drunk Drivers
Knoxville, Tenn.

KEEP YOUR LIGHTS ON BY DOING THE FOLLOWING:

1. Recall where you lived, what kind of work your mother and father did, who your playmates were, and what kind of fun things you enjoyed when you were eight to 10 years old. Remember the house where you lived.
2. As you think about your life as a child, consider the three things you passionately wanted, but didn't get.
3. List the way those deprivations affect your behavior today.
4. Resolve that the child inside you will not control you.
5. Let your childhood experiences help you better understand yourself and become more sensitive to others.
6. Remember, you are in charge. You are a victim of your past only when you let yourself be.
7. Consider the behavior characteristics you see in others and think about what some of their childhood experiences might have been.

WORKSHEET 4
GETTING IN TOUCH WITH MY CHILD WITHIN

This four-step exercise will help you get in touch with the child within you. Then you can discover how this child still influences you and your behavior today.

Step 1:

What was your childhood like when you were eight to 10 years old?

____

____

____

____

____

____

____

____

Step 2:

Name all the things you remember wanting, but not getting, when you were eight to 10 years old.

____

____

____

____

____

____

____

Step 3:

Select three items from your list of "wants" when you were eight to 10 years old. Write them below as your "most wanted" list for when you were young.

____

____

____

Step 4:

In what ways have these unmet wants influenced your life?

____

____

____

____

____

____

____

____

____

____

5

What Do You Like About You?

In the movies, comedian Bob Hope would often look in the mirror, pat his hair, moisten his eyebrows, and with a self-appreciative smile, proclaim, "You good-looking devil!" We found that funny because it was unexpected. We expected modesty; we got what we assumed to be conceit. Our parents had raised us better than that!

Yet I've discovered that the more we appreciate our good qualities, the less likely we are to be self-centered, uncaring, domineering—qualities no one admires.

The Rev. John Powell, S.J., one of the most published Christian authors alive today, is one of my literary and personal heroes. His books have greatly shaped and molded who I am today. They opened for me new windows of understanding that continue to enrich me in my quest to be all that God designed me to be.

I first met Father Powell in Kansas City at a seminar he was conducting. Later, I did a three-day seminar myself for a group of State Farm managers in Chicago. I'd conducted many seminars for my company throughout North America, but going to Chicago proved to be a highlight of my company career. There, just as I had everywhere else, I mentioned the great impact of John Powell's writings on my life.

The host of that particular conference wanted to give me something special as a thank-you gift. So he called Loyola University to ask if Powell might be able to see his No. 1 fan. Father Powell had an hour open that afternoon.

At the appointed time, I entered Powell's office for my personal visit with a man whose insightful writings had richly touched my life. After telling him so, I shared with him the basic concept of my "Keep Your Lights On" presentations. I gave him a KYLO pin for his lapel and a KYLO baseball cap.

Powell affirmed what he understood about "Keep Your Lights On," He even said, "It's a journey to begin, even if you never finish it." Then he asked, "Tom, what do you like about you?" Not wishing to seem conceited, I stuttered and stammered. Finally, I confessed that I didn't know how to answer his question, had never really thought about it.

Powell, ever the sensitive, caring person that he is, suggested that I make a list of the qualities that I liked about Tom Gunnels. He confessed that he had a list of more than 250 things that he liked about himself. Needless to say, I began my list on the taxicab ride back to the Chicago hotel where I was staying!

WHAT I LIKE ABOUT ME

Between then and now, I have identified 80 things I like about Tom Gunnels. Here are just a few of the items on my list. (Probably by now you're absolutely sure that I'm going to ask you to make just such a list! Well, you're right!)

WHAT I LIKE ABOUT TOM GUNNELS

- my height
- my general appearance
- my personality
- my speaking voice
- my empathy with others
- my role as a parent, grandparent, and husband
- my care for my first wife during her long illness
- my persistency
- my dogged determination
- my ability to dream, to inspire, and to be inspired
- my continual search for personal growth and development
- my success as an insurance manager
- my success as a speaker
- my success as a writer
- my ability to help others see themselves in a positive way
- my writing skills

- my ability to encourage and to be encouraged
- my ability to challenge my own thinking
- my willingness to say I'm sorry
- my work with a wide variety of organizations
- my involvement in my church
- my level of giving to church and charity
- my success in developing several outstanding insurance agents
- my work with an agent involved in drug abuse
- my ability to communicate
- my ability to face life as it is
- my ability to relate to children
- my ability to resist having an opinion on every subject

My list goes on. Each day provides new opportunities to expand it. I can continue to add to my list because I'm not through with my life. I haven't done all I can do or all I care to do. My life goes on, and I'm continuing to grow. So my list grows with me.

Sometimes, just like everyone else, I grow weary of doing something. When I'm on that downward road that leads to nowhere, I pull out my things-I-like-about-me list. It evokes memories of accomplishments and satisfactions that regenerate my enthusiasm, renew my zest, and get me back on the road to recovery.

In short order, I tackle the task before me with a renewed determination to see it through. Why am I able to begin again? Because my list reminds me of what I have done in the past. If I could do that then, I can do even more now!

At the end of 1994, I underwent surgery at Vanderbilt Hospital in Nashville for cancer of the prostate. Admittedly, there have been and likely will continue to be difficult moments associated with my recovery. The usual problems involving incontinence and impotence were bothersome. Sometimes I had the feeling "Woe is me." I'm not proud of that, but it's true. That feeling contributed nothing to my well-being, and it's certainly not in keeping with someone who expects to keep his lights on.

It was precisely in those moments of depression that I needed to review my list of things I like about myself. I needed to reflect on the qualities I wanted to demonstrate then. What I wanted to do was to handle the aftermath of my cancer surgery so that I would later be proud of how I had responded to the challenge. What happened as a result of my surgery is that I became actively involved in the Wellness Community and in the American Cancer Society.

Part of what I like about me is that I used what some would call a roadblock—my illness—to grow into a more caring and responsible person. So now I'm adding new things to my list. I've looked at how I've handled specific events and seen things I can admire about myself. For instance:

- Late at night, traveling through Arkansas, my wife and I came upon two elderly ladies with a flat tire. I changed that tire. I like that about me.

- Another time, I went to a friend's small restaurant and found out that his waiter had not shown up for the heavy lunch crowd. I donned an apron and helped out. I like that about me.

- While I was a volunteer waiter, a man and two small girls came in. "We're hungry. Can you help us?" the man asked. I seated them, ordered lunch for them, and paid the bill without telling the owner. As they rose to leave, I put a $20 bill in the man's shirt pocket.

  Months later, that man went back to the restaurant and talked to the owner to learn the name of the man who wore a business suit under his apron. He gave the owner a $20 bill for me and a slip of paper. On the paper, the man had written only one word: "Thanks." He gave no name; he just thanked me.

  That touched me deeply. I like myself for helping him. And I hope that if he's writing a list today, he likes himself for what he did too.

My list of what I like about me goes on and on and on. Maybe someday it'll grow to 200 or more! Like John Powell's!

YOUR LIST OF WHAT YOU LIKE ABOUT YOURSELF

That's enough about me and my list! Now it's your turn. What do you like about you? Using Worksheet 5 on page 121, I'd like you to write down all the qualities, traits, and actions that you truly like about yourself.

Start your list now. Don't limit yourself only to wonderful qualities, but include how well you handled specific events. Reflect on some of your past behaviors that make your proud. List them. Be specific.

Be assured that your list will bless you many times over, just as mine has done. Each time you review it, each time you add something new to it, you will realize how much there is in you to like.

One of the great truths of human nature is that we behave in a manner consistent with how we feel about ourselves. The better you feel about you, the better your attitude and your behavior toward others. And the more you love yourself, the more you can love others.

So look at yourself and your life. Find those things you want to commend about yourself. You are not being egotistical, you are liking yourself. If you don't like you, how can anyone else?

KEEP YOUR LIGHTS ON BY DOING THE FOLLOWING:

1. Remember that liking yourself is not being conceited or egotistical.
2. Make a list of the qualities, traits, actions, qualities you like about yourself.
3. For your own self-encouragement, review this list often.
4. Make additions to your list as you find new things to like about yourself.
5. Remember that the list is only for you, not for anyone else.
6. Accept the truth that you can love others only when you love yourself.

WORKSHEET 5
WHAT I LIKE ABOUT MYSELF

Make a list of the qualities, traits, and actions you like about yourself. To do this, think of all you have accomplished during your life. Think of all you do for others. Think of the way you are, the way you act, the way you relate to other people. All of this will help you get in touch with your admirable qualities, traits, and actions.

6

Your Time Line— Past and Future

As I said in earlier chapters, getting in touch with your past provides a road map for the present and the future. At the end of this chapter, you will prepare a time line of your life. Why a time line? Because it helps you see your past growth. A time line does the following:

- It provides an historical perspective of what you have done, lived through, enjoyed and celebrated.
- It gives other family members a picture of some of the challenges you have faced and the success you have achieved at certain moments in your life.
- It increases your current resolve by helping you remember how you have handled a myriad of challenges and opportunities in your past.

Once again, I'm going to show you how I filled out my time line. I share my own experiences with you so that you will find the exercise easier to understand and to complete. A quick look at my own time line will give you the kind of information you'll want to consider.

TOM GUNNELS' TIME LINE FOR THE PAST

1929: Born in Hanover, Texas, in Milam County. Father owned a country combination grocery-service-station-blacksmith-shop store.

1934: Hit in head with a baseball bat when I walked across home plate as the batter swung at the ball. Doctor told parents I'd never be normal.

1935: First grade at Hanover's two-room school house. Later, from my fifth through my sophomore year, attended Milano, a consolidated system that served most of Milam County.

1937: Mother dies after a long illness. She had a kidney infection, complicated by pregnancy.

1944: Dad's grocery store fails. Farm workers—customers—moved away to work in the defense plants. Dad, then age forty-seven, pulled up stakes, moved to Freeport, and worked for Dow. (We lived briefly in

Galveston when Dad worked at the shipyards. We also lived a short while in Temple where we operated a barbecue restaurant.) My first job: Krause's Bakery. Freeport High School was a life-changing event for me. Katharine Street, my algebra teacher and counselor, had a tremendous influence on me. She changed my life.

1945: Promoted to Head Baker at Krause's.

1946: Graduated from high school. Worked briefly as sales manager for Krause's Appliance Co. Entered U.S. Air Force with best friend Don Palmer.

1947: Air Force sent me to Guam. Promoted to corporal, then sergeant. In spare time, founded squadron newspaper, *17th Communiqué;* also founded the Guam Armed Forces Press Association, which was integrated prior to the rest of AF. First trip to Tokyo as a courier of top secret encoding equipment. In Tokyo met a Col. Mahoney, ATC Commander, who took a special interest in me because of my shyness over my missing tooth. He arranged for me to be billeted in Tokyo proper and took me to see General MacArthur. On a soldiers' picnic at Tumon Bay, rescued from near drowning by best friend Zim Jernigan.

1948: Promoted to S/Sgt. Outstanding Airman award trip to Tokyo.

1949: Discharged from U.S. Air Force in August. G.I. Bill enabled me to enroll at SMU. Developed laundry-dry cleaning route with four employees. Later worked at Central Freight Lines loading trailers. Then worked at Lee Way Motor Freight Lines, first as a billing clerk, later as rate clerk with charge of the billing unit. Bought first car—a 1946 Nash. Later, bought a new 1950 Nash.

1950: Met Sue in September. Engaged in December with plans to marry in 1953.

1951: Sue and I decide to marry sooner—June 3. Bought '52 Nash.

1954: Graduated from SMU. State Farm hired me as personnel manager trainee. Began in home office in Bloomington, Ill. In August, appointed personnel manager for new regional office in Murfreesboro, Tenn. Responsible for three states.

1955: Built first new home. New regional office opened in April. My department started employee newspaper—SCOPE; opened medical unit; set up suggestion system and education and training program; employed an educational consultant; established employees' activities-recreational association funded by company per-capita contribution plus the profits from all vending machines.

1957: Susan born April 29. (Sue decided we should start our family when my salary hit $450 a month.) When Susan was six months old, Sue went to work for General Electric as personnel secretary. She loved that job. (We had a full-time house worker to care for Susan.)

1958: Promoted to company's first agency training director. With that promotion, Sue and I decided to conceive our second child. Salary was nearing $8,000 annually. (Bought a '57 Mercury; kept '52 Nash.)

1959: Promoted to agency manager, Knoxville, following that district's loss of 22 percent of the policyholders in one year. Sandra was born July 5.

1960: Appointed 10 agents, most ever by one manager in one year.

1961: Sue's illness began, diagnosed terminal in April. In August, we went to NYC to see a noted neurologist. He diagnosed her as having a vitamin B-1 deficiency. He was mistaken. In November, Sue entered National Institute of Health, Bethesda. Appointed six agents. (First SF manager to appoint 16 agents in two years.)

1932

Left to right: Jean, Tom, and Talmadge in front of father's shop.

1933

Left to right: T.P., Jean, Talmadge, Tom, Jim in mother's arms, and Alice.

TIME LINE

1944
Family moves to Freeport, Texas. Left to right: Jim, Tom, T.P., stepmother Ruby, and stepsister Chris.

1945
Tom, head baker for Krause's Bakery, Freeport.

1952
Military Ball. Sue and Tom, Cadet Major USAF ROTC at SMU.

1962: Appointed two agents. Sue left NIH, later went to Vanderbilt several times, all without benefit. Traded in both cars for a '62 Chevrolet. Sue no longer can drive.

1963: Appointed two agents. Succession of housekeepers hired. Susan entered first grade as Sue proudly watched her enter school's front door, said prayer of thanksgiving for being alive to witness that proud moment.

1964: Sue's illness began to claim her eyesight. Walking became more difficult. Took family vacation by plane (a luxury then), knowing it would be Sue's last trip. She took last unaided steps at Atlanta airport while we were en route home. Appointed three agents. Fred Harb became region's top agent. Bought color TV because Sue couldn't see black and white. Celebrated Christmas knowing it was our last one together. Susan and Sandra got their first bikes. We had each one's name painted on her bike.

1965: Sue died August 2. Sandra entered first grade. Harb became region's first $1,000,000 life producer, fifth in the company.

1966: Flew first cross country after getting my pilot's license. Minor, but potentially serious, accident at Birmingham airport.

1967: Appointed one agent.

1968: Appointed one agent. Girl Scouts national magazine, *The Leader*, publishes my "Thank Heaven for Little Girls."

1969: Appointed one agent. Two agents qualified for life leaders club. We were one of only 18 in all of State Farm to qualify more than one. We also recorded the first $1,000,000 life month in our region. Senior agent D.J. Maynard died.

1970: Married Frankie August 16. Became president of Convention Bureau.

1971: Appointed two agents. Chaired Chamber's "We're Glad You're Here" campaign.

1972: To Madrid with Frankie—State Farm trip.

1973: Became president of Better Business Bureau. Appointed one agent. Qualified as a life leader manager for the first time. To Munich with Frankie—State Farm trip.

1974: To Paris with Susan, Sandra, and Frankie—State Farm trip. To Costa Del Sol, Spain, with Frankie—State Farm trip.

1975: Appointed three agents. Susan entered SMU. Agent John Dunlap dies after a brief illness. Family vacationed in Mexico City and Acapulco. To Maui, Hawaii, with Frankie—State Farm trip.

1976: Elected to SMU Dad's Club Board. District sets new life insurance record by producing more than $2 million in each of two consecutive months. We also set a new company record for most new fire premiums in one month. To Bahamas with Frankie—SF trip.

1977: Chaired RVP Billips' retirement program. Family vacationed in Vienna. To Acapulco with Frankie—SF trip.

1978: Susan married Ben Terrill. *Life Association News* published my article "To CLU or Not to CLU."

1979: Appointed two agents. To Monte Carlo with Frankie—SF trip.

1980: To Maui with Frankie—SF trip.

1981: Appointed one agent. Purchased '82 Cadillac. To Montreal with Frankie—SF trip.

1982: Sandra marries Lacy Harville. To Disney World with Frankie—SF trip.

1983: Appointed two agents. SF award trip to Munich.

1984: District hosted surprise luncheon honoring my 30th year with SF. To Maui with Frankie—SF trip. Grandson Matt Terrill born in June. Purchased '85 Cadillac.

1985: Appointed two agents. To Acapulco with Frankie—SF trip.

1986: Appointed two agents. Devised Gunnels Work Units Formula; copyrighted it. Also developed Promotion Index, along with Value of One and Value of Ten. District recorded region's first $1 million+ new fire premium year. SF trip to Disney World.

1987: Represented region at corporate managers' planning conference. State Farm's home office sent film crew to make video—"A Manager's Staff, Systems and Facilities"—for companywide distribution. To Bermuda with Frankie—SF trip. Granddaughter Melissa Terrill born in August.

1988: Appointed one agent. Was guest manager-instructor for Colorado region. Also, instructor for Managers' Leadership Seminars for State Farm in San Diego, Bloomington, Toronto, Florida. Purchased '89 Lincoln. Granddaughter Lauren Harville born in December.

1989: To Maui with Frankie—SF trip. Speaker at Houston ALU. *Leaders* magazine publishes my "Winners are Self-Made."

1990: Guest manager-instructor for Nebraska and Michigan regions. President Knoxville ALU. Also, honored with KALU's man of the year award. President for National

Conference of Christians and Jews. *Leaders* magazine publishes my "Guaranteed Ways to Lose."

1991: Rotarian of the Year, Downtown Rotary. Agency representative in planning RVP Pope's retirement. Took cruise with Frankie—SF trip.

1992: Met author John Powell when my son-in-law Ben Terrill and I attended his Kansas City weekend conference. Grandson Conner Harville born in April.

1993: Conducted SF seminars in Chicago and Lake Geneva. Met with John Powell in his office at Loyola U. He encouraged me to pursue my KYLO. Purchased '94 Cadillac. To Maui—SF trip.

1994: To Vienna with Frankie—SF trip. Prostate cancer diagnosed in September. Prior to surgery in November, Frankie and I enjoy a five-day holiday in New York City. Also, a family reunion the week before my surgery in November.

1995: Made decision in March to retire at the end of August. To Bermuda with Frankie—SF trip. Received Brotherhood Award from NCCJ. Started Tom Gunnels Seminars on Sept. 1. Conducted seminars for International Technologies and Mt. Sterling Chamber of Commerce in Kentucky.

1996: Started writing manuscript of KYLO. Seminars for John Daniel Clothing Company; Allstate Insurance; Blue Ridge Leadership Conference; Tennessee Association Plumbing, Heating, Cooling Contractors; State of Tennessee Treasury Department; First Tennessee Bank; Memphis ALU; Episcopal Laymen's Conference. Author John Powell suggested I send KYLO manuscript to Thomas More Publishing in Allen, Texas. KYLO required many rewrites before I was satisfied with it. Worked hard on learning to live with consequences of prostate cancer surgery. Became active in American Cancer Society and the Wellness Community. Mailed KYLO manuscript to Thomas More on December 26.

1997: Had several discussions and two visits with Thomas More executives. Led to contract signed in my office on October 3. Conducted several seminars for State Farm in Colorado. State of Tennessee booked KYLO for third group. May be booked for fourth. Stepped up promotion of seminars in preparation for KYLO publication. Began *Lights for the Journey,* a series of books as a companion to KYLO. Worked on books for children.

1965
Sandra, 6, Susan, 8, and Tom, a couple of months after Sue's death.

1976
Receiving award from W.W. Billips, Tom is named one of State Farm's top 10 regional managers.

Time Line

1995

Tom and Frankie with grandchildren.
Matt, 11, and Melissa, 8, are on the left;
Lauren, 7, and Conner, 3, are on the right.

1995

Tom accepts the
State Farm
Life Achievement
Award.

1996

Mr. KYLO
in snow at
Lake Clark,
Alaska.

TOM GUNNELS' TIME LINE FOR THE FUTURE

I have also written a time line for my future. These are the events that I look forward to. I visualize their happening; I picture myself doing these things. I've discovered that when I dream big, big things happen. My dreaming prompts my acting. So I don't content myself with dreaming about my rowboat coming in. I picture an ocean liner smoothly cruising into the harbor of my life!

Here are the entries I've made in my future time line for 1998 and 1999. But believe me, I'm well into the year 2000 and beyond already!

1998: *Keep Your Lights On* to be published in spring '98. Appear on national TV promoting book, seminars. Seminar company to be running full blast. New books being produced. New staff members hired, including an administrative assistant. The book *Sue's New Shoes* to be under contract during the year. Trip for Frankie and me to Alaska or back to England.

1999: Seminar company to need more than one presenter this year. Expect to be promoting single event seminars in major cities. Trips in future years—an extended trip to the American West; visits to Shanghai, Singapore, and Tokyo. Be in a stage play.

MIRACLES IN MY TIME LINE

I believe that all of us are the products of a series of miracles. You'll note in my time-line entry for 1934, that I got hit in the head. During a sandlot baseball game, I unexpectedly walked across home plate just as the hitter swung at the ball. The bat caught me behind my left ear, sending me into a coma that lasted four days. Medicine couldn't do much for me then. The doctor told my parents, "If he survives, he'll have to be institutionalized for the rest of his life." (Now I ask you: Do you have as good an excuse as I do for being somewhat "strange"?) I count that as a miracle!

When I look at my dad's life and at my family life, I see other miracles. For example: In 1902, when my dad was five, he was walking behind a mule that was blind in one eye. Dad startled the animal, and it kicked him in the head. For the rest of his life, Dad carried the outline of that horseshoe on his forehead. His injury was severe, but Dad's family lived a day's wagon ride from the doctor, so his family treated him at home as best they knew how.

Dad hovered near death for several days and was seriously injured for weeks. But eventually he made a full recovery. I consider that a miracle. My dad survived. If he hadn't, I wouldn't be here!

Then, when I was five, I survived being hit in the head. That's another miracle! Without that miracle, my two daughters and their children would not be alive.

Other miracles have occurred in my family. In 1966, in my first cross-country trip as a private pilot, with my daughters on board, a wreck at the Birmingham airport could have wiped us all out. Miracle No. 3! A grandson had to have his stomach pumped when he was two, after ingesting a toxic amount of Tylenol. Miracle No. 4!

The unbroken chain continues.

YOUR TIME LINE

Now you can begin to write your own time lines—for your past life and one for your future! Use Worksheet 6 on page 143 to get you started and think of your entries as just hitting the high spots. But if your time lines are going to be as long as mine, then I suggest that you type them on a computer or typewriter!

For your past time line, start with the time and place of your birth. Include the highlight years when you reached each new plateau. Remember to record some of the heartaches and obstacles. Why? Because they'll remind you of your ability to meet life as it really is, which is not always as you wish it to be.

As you write your time line, remember the person you used to be and embrace that person. Feel love and compassion and empathy toward that person. That's how I feel about the little boy who got hit with a bat when he was four.

And as you write your time line, consider the miracles that have occurred in your life. Put them on your time line. Rejoice in them. Also, please recognize the obvious: As long as you live, you can add to your time line. You can add not only what you visualize for the future, but what you remember of the past.

After completing your past time line for this chapter, you'll read it over and you'll remember even more. Then, as time passes you'll recollect other important events from your life. You'll learn even more when you consult other sources of information within your family.

On Worksheet 6, I ask you to think about your past and to dream for your future. Visualize what you'd like to happen for you in the next few years. What do you want to achieve? Where would you like to travel? What would you like to happen for your family?

Make a future time line by dreaming about what's going to happen next for you!

KEEP YOUR LIGHTS ON BY DOING THE FOLLOWING:

1. To discover your personal history and enhance your person perspectives, write a time line of your life.
2. Make additions to your time line as you remember new things and as time passes and new events touch your life.
3. Remember that your family members will appreciate the information your time line contains about you and your challenges and successes.
4. Be assured that "there is more yet to come."
5. Create a future time line and keep adding to it. Remember that having things you plan and want to do enhances your quality of living.

WORKSHEET 6
MY PERSONAL TIME LINE

Step 1

To discover your personal history and enhance your personal perspectives, write a time line of your past life. Start your time line by listing major events and dates that have significantly influenced or defined you.

Step 2

Create a future time line. List several items, events, or achievements you want in your future. Dream big!

Getting in Touch with
Your Present

7

Your Vision Is Your Personal Mission

We have only one shot at life. In fact, we have only one shot at today, tomorrow, the rest of our life! When this day, this month, this year, this life is gone, we can do absolutely nothing to change anything that happened. We had one shot; we took it; it's gone. So, let's make our one shot a hole in one! Let's keep our lights on!

Another way to say this is that we are not in a dress rehearsal for life. We are acting in a one-nighter! We don't have an extended run to try over and over to get our lines right. We're not practicing; we're actually presenting the play! So let's make our role worth a Tony, an Oscar, an Emmy! Let's keep our lights on!

One way to ensure that we take a masterful shot and play a winning role is to write a personal mission statement. This chapter explains the why and how of that.

WHY NOT ALL OF YOU?

All of us fall short of what we might become. Some of us fear that if we reach a new plateau, others will expect us to repeat a similar level or, worse, to exceed the one we reached. We end up never even trying. Why? Because if we never reach that level, we'll never have to do more.

Roger Bannister, the first person to run a four-minute mile, had to overcome that inner holding back. He heard the voice within say, "Don't run it once, you'll be expected to do it all over again." Because he did not succumb to that temptation, he left a legacy to all athletes who came after him.

The question each of us faces is "Why not all of me, not just a part of me? Why not all that I am as parent, spouse, worker, church member, citizen in my community?"

When I first wrote my personal mission statement, I imagined the following conversation that might occur when I meet my Maker. In this visualization, I'm waiting to be checked in. God approaches. "Son, I have just one question to ask: Why were you not all of you? Why only part of you, in all areas of your life?"

"All of me?" I ask, getting nervous and stalling for time so I can come up with my best answer.

Then, with complete authority and resoluteness, God speaks again, "Yes, Tom. Again I ask, why not all of you?"

"Well, I did pretty well, didn't I? I wasn't all that bad, was I?"

"No, son, you weren't all that bad, and you did pretty well. "But, you're not answering my question: Why not all of you?"

Again, I'm in the defensive mode. "Well, I was thoughtful, considerate, maybe even above average for those in my neighborhood and family."

"Why don't you want to answer my question? I know you hear it. Why did you choose to be less than I designed you to be? I want to hear your answer."

At this moment I know that I must answer. Somewhere I'm hoping my fertile imagination will jump in with something clever to say. In the meantime, I'm hearing, "Tom, why do you think I sent those folks in your balcony to show you the way? Why did I give you an intellect, sensitive emotions, dreams? Why did I give you talents? Why did I give you so much time? Surely you've wondered why? You didn't think it was all just a happenstance, with no purpose? Again, Tom, I want an answer—why not all of you?"

I'm desperate now as I say, "Wait a minute. May I ask a question?"

"Of course, you may ask a question. But asking a question is not the same as answering one."

"You mentioned my talents, my intellect, my time, and also my dreams. I'm confused. Where did those dreams come from?"

"Come now," God says. "You must know. Your dreams of who and what you could be were my gifts to you. Do you know what your gift to me is? It's what you did with those dreams. You see, a dream is just another window that's opened to expose new light, new hope. It was precisely when you were dreaming of possibilities that I was getting messages through to you, giving you an idea of what you might do, what you might become. Yes, my son, those dreams came from me."

"Oh, my God!"

The silence is broken with one perfect and powerful word: "Yes?"

"I didn't know, I didn't realize." I feel bad as I frame another question, "May I have another shot at it? May I try again?"

The answer is not to my liking. "No, my son. You had your chance. That's the way it works. No repeats. After all, life's not a dress rehearsal."

I had that imaginary conversation with God many years ago. Fortunately, I still have time to prepare an acceptable answer to the question that God will surely ask: "Why not all of you?"

We do not need to climb the highest mountain, we just need to keep climbing our own mountain. And all of us do have our own mountains to climb—somewhere, somehow. Hopefully, we are improving our mountain-climbing abilities as we seek to become all that God has designed us to be.

MY PERSONAL MISSION STATEMENT

Establishing my personal mission was a defining moment for me. I reasoned that since all responsible organizations have mission statements, so should I. My church had one; State Farm, where I worked, had one; the Civic Club to which I belonged had one. In fact, every community and service organization that I knew about had a mission statement. They knew what they sought to be and to become. Surely, I reasoned, if it's important for organizations to define their basic mission, then it's important for me too.

I wrote my personal mission statement more than 20 years ago. As I prepared to put it on paper, I looked backward on the life I had already lived and forward to the one I wanted to live. I wanted to write a mission statement that would become a beacon to light my path toward my future. The statement would tell me what I was to become. Knowing that, I would make certain choices, grab certain opportunities, say certain things, act in a certain way. I'd do all I had to do to become who I wanted to be.

As I wrote my mission statement, I took into account a simple truth: when I meet my Maker, God will not ask me why I was not Abraham or David or the Messiah. Rather, God will ask, "Why were you not Tom? Tom Gunnels? All of Tom, not just part of him?"

Believing that I must be all of me, I wrote the following personal mission statement: "Someday, I want to meet Tom, all of Tom, not just part of him." My shorter version became "Be all of Tom."

Proudly I proclaim that I am still in the course of developing Tom. My best is still ahead of me. I have not yet arrived. I'm still on the journey to become all that God designed me to be.

True, I have made considerable progress, but as much progress as I have made, I have more to do to become a fully realized Tom Gunnels. I want to know more about me. I want to know what possibilities exist within me.

I know I have no second shots at living this life. Therefore, I want to make this shot count. Will I fail in the future in spite of my resolve? Probably. But this much is certain—I'll get back up and keep on trying. I'll do this for my own sake. But I'll also get back up for the sake of those who are watching and learning from me. If I'm going to set an example, and I will, then I want that example to be a good one.

The improvement I seek in me is not restricted to my profession, my job, my work. It includes all of me, in all facets of my life. I want to be all of Tom as a person, a spouse, a parent, a grandparent, a worker in my church, a citizen in my community. All of me, period.

Both in my first career and in my second, I have embraced the concept of continuous improvement. In my first career, this concept became the cornerstone of my management philosophy. I believe that as long as we make annual improvement, we will continue along the way to truly great performance.

When I first used this concept in sales management, the conventional wisdom was to get salespeople to compete against each other for supremacy. I felt that provided only one winner; I wanted everyone to be a winner. (Years after I began to use the concept of continuous improvement, I learned that Edward Deming was the first to introduce it to business. The idea became the core of his monumental work with the Japanese.)

Holding on to this philosophy, I appointed and developed some outstandingly successful people in the insurance business. I never suggested that anyone of them should try to outsell or outproduce anyone else. I simply encouraged each to beat himself or herself, to make an improvement each year, to be open to new ideas, to experiment, and to innovate. I frequently asked one question: "Have you had your best year yet, your best month?"

Once, and only once, one of my associates told me that his best was behind him. It was a heartrending moment for both of us. He was a special friend who had achieved greatly and whose generous heart and spirit touched many people, particularly me. We enjoyed our association with each other, and both of us appreciated the gifts of time, talent, and energy that God had given us.

This man was one of those rare people who are true to their word, who live up to their best, who are willing to go the second mile, who choose to be responsible and accountable. Born into extreme poverty, with only a high-school education, he had built a business generating more than $1.5 million in premiums.

When he said, "Tom, my best is behind me," I knew he was speaking the hard truth. He was still at work, but he suffered from advanced emphysema. Only a portable oxygen supply kept him going. "Oh, how I wish," he continued, "that my best was still ahead of me. But it isn't."

I looked him in the eye to give him the affirmation he had richly earned. "But your best has been tremendous, Edwin. Whatever was needed, you did. You've been a positive influence in my life—on all of us privileged to work with you. Your best may be behind you, but your best will be a beacon for me for all of my years to come."

As I left his office, I vowed to be all of Tom, just as Edwin had been all of Edwin. I vowed to keep my best ahead of me for as long as health and life permitted. On that day I renewed my personal mission statement. I read it out loud to myself: "Someday, I want to meet Tom, all of Tom, not just part of him." Like a mantra, I whispered the shorter version to myself: "Be all of Tom."

YOUR PERSONAL MISSION STATEMENT

Believe me, you are in charge of who you are and where you are going! Obviously, accepting personal responsibility for your own present and future makes you accountable. And that's an essential ingredient if you want to maximize your personal growth. In fact, until you accept responsibility and become accountable, you treat yourself as a victim. That term implies that you bear no personal responsibility or accountability.

To make your own lights shine as brightly as they can, you must cease to blame your past, your parents, your prior education, your spouse, your boss. Get on with your life by saying, "I am responsible for who I am and for where I am going. Period." From now on, take responsibility for your own actions, your own dreams, your own life. Accept the consequences of your decisions and move forward.

You are on a lifelong journey. You may never reach the far-flung destination you have for yourself. That truly is not important. What is important is the journey, the striving, the reaching. These are worth everything you can give.

You won't get where you want to go in one giant leap. You will need to take one step at a time. An old Chinese proverb says that a journey of a thousand miles begins with a single step. Take that step. Embrace the concept of continuous improvement. A better you, a more fully realized you, is eager to get out. Let that better you out, not for your benefit alone, but for all the world to see!

I encourage you to use Worksheet 7 on page 158 to write your own mission statement. Write so concisely, so clearly, that generations from now those who read it will know clearly who it is you sought to become with your time and your talents. Your task is to start today the process that will allow you to define the course your life will take from now on.

As you write your mission statement, ask yourself why you are not all that God has designed you to be. You have time, opportunities, and talents. The people in your balcony have provided the illumination you need. What will you do with all these gifts? Who will you become?

The question today is "What is your mission? What are you all about?" As you write your answer on Worksheet 7, be aware that this is only your first effort. You will probably not get the words exactly as you want them. That's okay. Just as you have to work at life, so you have to work at honing your mission statement until it says precisely who you dream of becoming.

Ideally, in the weeks and months and years ahead, you'll revisit your statement many times and revise it often. Continuous improvement is the name of the game.

Neither you nor I have to beat anybody. All we have to do is improve, get better each year. We must strive to improve our prior efforts and to become all that we can be. We can become the vision that God has of us.

Letter from "Keep Your Lights On" Seminar

Every business person should hear and heed the "Keep Your Lights On" message. Your KYLO principles will be helpful to the youngster just starting or to someone who has been around the block. KYLO sets the path toward success and satisfaction. Thanks.

Mr. Russell Perry, CLU,
Life insurance sales for
62-plus years

KEEP YOUR LIGHTS ON BY DOING THE FOLLOWING:

1. Remember: You have only one shot at life, so make it a hole in one! You're not in a dress rehearsal. You're actually acting in the one performance of this play called your life!
2. Make your personal vision into your personal mission.
3. Ask yourself, "Why do I hold back becoming all that my talents would permit?"
4. Be prepared to answer the following question that God will ask, "Why were you not you?"
5. Embrace the concept of continuous improvement.

WORKSHEET 7
MY PERSONAL MISSION STATEMENT

Write your personal mission statement. Who do you want to become? Who do you want to be for yourself and for those who see you as their model, teacher, example of how to live?

As you do this, remember that life is lived in a constant stage of editing and revising. Be willing to change your responses as you gain new insights and understanding about who you and where you're going.

8

Your Core Values

At your very core is the real you. When you know your core, you'll discover more of the real you than you ever imagined. If you are not, at this moment, certain what your core is, rest easy. Many people go through life unable to define their core values. You need not, and must not, fall into that category, because you *can* find your core values.

In finding them, you find a way to help you keep your lights on! This chapter shows you how.

Learning from Business

Every well-run business defines its core values. A business does this by setting policies that govern its day-to-day operations. In the personnel arena, for example, every business establishes its core values with regard to sick leave, vacation, and salary administration. The business designs its policy statements to govern 99 percent of the situations that arise in the course of its operation. The remaining 1 percent will require individual judgment based on the facts of the specific case.

In the main, however, well-run businesses establish their core values to govern their day-to-day actions, which should reflect the standards they have set. Organizations that have defined their core values are more consistent and predictable as they respond to various circumstances in the course of their business. In so doing, they introduce order and measured comfort to all involved in the enterprise.

These policy directives are "statements of intention" that should apply approximately 99 percent of the time. In short, they are what the business intends to do, not necessarily what will be done in all cases. Companies allow deviations under circumstances that can be documented and defended. The "99 percent rule" is itself an intention, but it is also a standard by which to measure the application of the policy.

State Farm Insurance Companies—for whom I worked 41 years—provides a good example of an established core value. In its manual, the company directors wrote the following: "We desire to pay every claim we owe for the amount we owe, not intentionally more and not intentionally less." All claims handling procedures flow from that stated corporate core value. This empowers the claims departments—and other support functions—to implement programs and procedures to fulfill that stated objective.

All well-run companies have statements that reflect their core values. The policy statements of General Electric, General Motors, General Dynamics, and General Tire define who they are and how they are going to respond to a variety of circumstances. A study of their policy statements yields a sense of who they are and what they are all about.

Hyram W. Smith, CEO of Franklin Quest Company, wrote the best-selling book, *The 10 Natural Laws of Successful Time and Life Management.*

In his book, Smith detailed Ben Franklin's experience with having established his core values early in life. More than 50 years after setting down his values, Franklin evaluated how they had benefited him and his accomplishments. (As reported in Smith's book, Ben Franklin observed that he did not follow his values 100 percent of the time.)

Smith's book led me to examine my own life and to establish my core values. So here's a list of my core values. Once again, I give it to you as an example in the hope that it will help you when you use Worksheet 8 on page 168, to write down your own core values.

TOM GUNNELS' CORE VALUES

The following are the benchmarks by which I desire to evaluate my behavior—past, present, and future. In all cases, I desire to live my life:

1. To earn the respect of those with whom I love, live, and work.

2. To be a source of encouragement, support, and strength to my wife, my daughters, my sons-in-law, and my grandchildren.

3. To seek financial security through my work achievements and by the prudent management of my resources.

4. To have my grandchildren know and value that I found them a joy and that I wanted to be an important part of their lives.

5. To be a faithful, responsive custodian of the trust and privilege accorded to me in my association with the State Farm Insurance Companies.

6. To be responsive in a meaningful and orderly way to the needs of others by my personal and economic support of the United Way and similar organizations that provide oversight and continuity to hurting, needing members of the community.

7. To continuously recognize the good in others and in myself and to celebrate these qualities to better enhance their growth in others and in myself.

8. To overcome adversity and difficulties with poise and perseverance so as to serve as a role model for others facing similar situations.

9. To hold myself accountable for my view of the world and to challenge my understanding by constant study and examination.

10. To seek to make a difference in all roles of my life—as a husband, parent, grandparent, churchman, insurance professional, and public speaker.

11. To reduce to writing some of the more meaningful experiences and lessons that have benefited me.

12. To seek continuous improvement so that I may move closer to becoming the kind of person my Maker designed me to be.

13. To encourage and uplift others in their journey in grateful appreciation to those who have similarly helped me.

14. To handle the aftermath of my cancer surgery so that if a grandson is similarly afflicted many years from now, he will, by remembering my example, know how he wants to handle himself and the situation.

I wished to be judged by these 14 core values. Admittedly, there may be circumstances that will dictate a departure from these intentions, but those situations should be rare. When they do arise, I will know that I am departing from my prescribed course of behavior.

And admittedly, I have had to add to these core values. A few years ago, following my diagnosis of cancer, I felt the need to add Number 14 to my list of core values. In the aftermath of a radical prostatectomy, meeting the challenges that followed suggested the need for an added guide. I needed one that would more specifically define my intended behavior in the light of my new circumstance. Core value Number 14 was the result.

YOU AND YOUR CORE VALUES

What about you? You also need well-defined benchmarks to guide your behavior. Your written core values say to the world, particularly your own personal world, that this is who you want to be. Both you and others can judge you by your own standards.

The set of principles you write on Worksheet 8 will enable you to handle future events in a way that reflects your core. These values indicate how you intend to live your life—not 100 percent of the time, but in the vast majority of situations as they arise.

As you begin to think about your core values, be assured that you are not binding yourself to only one way of acting. Quite the contrary. These values allow you to know when you are making exceptions. No rule, no policy statement, no core value can cover all circumstances.

A time may come when you will decide to contradict your core values, but you will regard that as the exception rather than the rule. At some other time, you may feel uncomfortable about your attitude or behavior in a certain situation. When that happens, you may be fairly certain that you are violating one of your core values.

By referring back to your written core values, you can readjust your behavior to be in accord with what you truly value. Thus you reintroduce inner harmony and accord into your life. You are being true to who you are and who you want to be.

An important reason for undertaking this task now is that you will be defining your values in the coolness of reflection, not in the heat of the moment. Calm reflection allows you to use your reason to establish how you want your behavior to be. Thus, you are more likely to define the kind of you that represents the way you truly want to live your life.

As you begin establishing your own core values, accept that the process of doing this is involved. Several weeks of trial and errors and re-examination will probably pass before you develop what defines your core. If, at the end of several weeks of reflection, you cannot define who you are, then accept that you need more self-examination.

So I encourage you to begin by rereading my list of core values and then jotting down your first thoughts on Worksheet 8. As the weeks pass, refine your first thoughts until you have a list that truly shows how you want to live your life.

When you are content and pleased with your list of core values, ask someone who knows you to assess your stated values to see if they represent the way that person has seen you live.

Remember: Having your own core beliefs carefully prepared in written form allows you to evaluate them whenever you wish and to modify them whenever your reasoned judgment dictates. Defining your values allows you to implement them more consistently and thoroughly than would be possible otherwise.

Throughout the rest of your life you want to live your core values. Living them enables you to keep your lights on!

KEEP YOUR LIGHTS ON BY DOING THE FOLLOWING:

1. Remember that at your very core is the real you, defined by your core values. These reflect the way you want to live your life.

2. Consult Hyram Smith's book, *The 10 Natural Laws of Successful Time and Life Management.*

3. Accept that if you cannot define who you are, you need more self-examination.

4. Rest assured that establishing your core values can help you move closer to becoming the kind of person your Maker designed you to be.

5. As your write your core values, realize that they provide a definition of who you are. Prepare a list that defines you

so well that anyone reading your values would know the kind of person you set out to be.

6. Ask someone who knows you to assess your stated values to see if they represent the way you have lived.
7. Acknowledge that you can and will deviate from your core values in unusual circumstances, but acknowledge, too, that these instances will be a rare exception.
8. Amend and add to your listed core values as you gain experience and encounter new circumstances.

WORKSHEET 8
MY CORE VALUES

What are the standards by which you wish to judge yourself? What are the standards by which you want others to judge you? What are the benchmarks by which you desire to evaluate your behavior—past, present, and future? How do you desire to live your life?

As you consider answers to these questions, begin to jot down the first core values that come to your mind.

In the days and weeks ahead, return to these first thoughts and refine them until you have a list that can guide your actions for the rest of your life.

9

Your Greatest Asset: Change

What's your greatest asset? That's a question I've asked thousands, individually and in my audiences. I'm sure that the answers I've received will sound familiar to you: "my wife," "my children," "my health." And all of these are worthy answers to such an important question.

However, the truth is, and always will be, that your greatest asset is your ability and willingness to change. Several decades ago, a learned conference of scholars from all disciplines sought to determine the greatest breakthroughs of the 20th century. They considered such far-reaching discoveries and inventions as penicillin, the jet engine, and atomic energy. Their list was long.

What did this learned group finally conclude? What is the greatest discovery of this century? That we can change. We can alter our circumstances by our own will and determination. We are not doomed to be who we think we are or who someone else may think we are. We can consciously and willfully change.

Yet a world of misinformation suggests the opposite. "We are basically who we are when we were four or five years of age," some will state with great authority. Hogwash!

"It's all in our genes." Hogwash again! We can't let ourselves hide behind such misbegotten notions.

The most dangerous six words in anyone's language are "That's just the way I am." This statement implies that we can do nothing about who we are or who we want to be. The fact is that we can change; we do change. Change is the major quality that separates winners from the also-rans.

Any of us who have learned a new discipline, like flying, or acquired new skills, like those of a surgeon, knows that we can learn and we can change. Of course, change can be difficult. Anyone who has ever quit a long-term habit like smoking knows just how difficult! To see how hard change can be try to quit something you do every day. Hard work!

But, obviously, change is not impossible because many of us have quit smoking; we have changed our habits and our lives. Why have some of us been able to change and others of us haven't? Because of motivation. When our motivation is strong, change in behavior and habits can and does occur. When motivated, we want to change. Without that desire, however, change can't and won't happen.

We can be unwilling to change, but that is vastly different from being unable to change. Change happens every day.

CHANGE I'VE EXPERIENCED

I've accomplished a great deal of change in my professional life. But in this chapter I want to limit myself to writing about only one change. Because I made that change, other changes farther down the line occurred to my benefit. (The lesson, of course, is that a change in one area introduces changes in other areas as well.)

My appointment as an agency manager—a manager of agents—came as an unwelcomed surprise. I wanted nothing to do with sales. Yet State Farm promoted me to a job I thought I could never do well.

Doing something I wanted to do seemed more desirable than changing and doing a new job for the company. But doing what we like doing isn't always possible. What's the next best thing then? Learning to like what we are doing. And, yes, we can do that. In fact, I not only learned to do my new job well, but I also learned to love doing it.

My prior inclination that I could not do that kind of work and would not enjoy doing it turned out to be grossly inaccurate. How much richer I am—and I believe others are also—because of my willingness to confront my own perceptions of my abilities.

For me, change involved hard work. That's the first ingredient of change. If we work hard, we generally come to love what we're doing. And if we do anything enough—say for 55 hours a week—we become good at it! Becoming good at it, we enjoy doing it. What happens all too often is that we don't give ourselves that chance. Instead of working hard at what we don't like doing, we work less. Then we never become proficient at what we do. Thus, we never learn to like doing it.

CHANGE I'VE ENCOURAGED

Early in my management career, I appointed Fred as an insurance sales agent for our company. Great guy. Hard worker. Ambitious. But he believed he couldn't change. Said so. One day, being very candid, he told me, "Tom, I'll never be able to sell life insurance. I just can't do that."

Yes, he knew the product. Yes, he could sell. Yes, he knew the sales presentations well. In fact, he was selling tons of casualty insurance. But for whatever reason, Fred saw himself as unable to sell a life product.

Knowing his perspective was all wet, I set out on a program to change Fred's way of looking at himself and his assets. I knew that I had to help him see himself in a more healthy, willing-to-change attitude. If I couldn't help him do that, then his prophecy about being unable to change would be self-fulfilling.

I began my campaign by arranging my schedule so that once a week I could spend some time with Fred, in an atmosphere as nonthreatening as I could make it. Over coffee and casual conversation, I started describing to Fred the qualities I saw in him.

I described his tenacity, his love for his family, his ability to establish rapport with the customer, his desire to always serve the needs of his customers, his willingness to be of service—all admirable qualities. He acknowledged that he believed he had those qualities. But still he had a blind spot in assessing his abilities to sell life insurance.

Next, I began to translate those qualities into achievement. I described his ability to help families evaluate their total insurance needs—including life insurance. I described him serving his clients in this way. I carefully emphasized the benefits that I could see accruing to Fred and to his clients, the honor and recognition that would come to him because of the results he was achieving. I stressed the respect that his customers and the company already felt for him. But Fred just shook his head from side to side.

One day, because my description of him was vastly different from his own self-perception, Fred, in sheer desperation, exclaimed, "I'd give anything if I could see the Fred you see."

There! My chance to make a difference in his life had finally come! Ready for the next step, I said, "Fred, I'm going to give you the opportunity to meet the Fred I know. But, first, you must agree to a couple of things."

"Okay," he said. "I'm willing to try."

"One, you must follow a specific plan we'll work out for at least 30 days. Two, you must keep an open mind. In return for that agreement, let me say that if in the next 30 days it turns out that you don't meet the Fred I know, then I'll quit bugging you about it."

"Deal," Fred enthusiastically agreed.

"Fine," I responded, "now here's the program. For the next 30 days, I want you to do nothing but sell life insurance. I know you think you can't sell it. But for 30 days, I want you to do nothing but sell what you think you can't sell. You'll have to work hard, make the calls, see the people, and report to me every day."

As some would say, "The rest is history." Not only did Fred discover that he could sell life insurance exceptionally well, he also came to love doing it. Having proved his ability to himself, within three years, he was leading our region of some 600 agents in selling life insurance.

The following year, Fred became one of the top five agents in our company of more than 17,000 agents. Three years after that, he started a five-year study program that earned a highly valued educational attainment—the CLU designation (Chartered Life Underwriter). By the time of his death in 1992, he had become a legend in our company because of his outstanding and remarkable life-insurance selling ability.

What's my point here? Fred's record achievement in this arena could not have occurred if he had not changed the way he viewed himself and his abilities. His change eventually led to wholesale changes in the training and expectations of our agency force. All of this was brought about because Fred discovered his greatest asset—his ability to change.

I'd like to share one more dimension to this remarkable story of change. Five years before I appointed him, Fred had undergone surgery to relieve back pain, a procedure that went awry. The operation left him in constant pain and greatly impaired his ability to walk. He could have qualified for permanent disability, but chose not to.

The fact that Fred began a new, demanding career and was able to embrace needed changes—in spite of his disability and in spite of his constant pain—is a story of great courage from which all of us can draw inspiration. When he died, he had endured more than 35 years of constant, untreatable pain. But in the last 30 years of his life, he had earned the reputation of being a leader in the selling of life insurance.

You and Change—Your Greatest Asset

Like Fred, you can choose to change. You can embrace new ideas, learn new skills, do more, be more. The limits you set on yourself, for whatever reason, become self-disabling. Leave your disabilities at the door and come into a bright sunshiny room, full of hope, promise, and change. Refuse to limit yourself! Accept change! Toss away your belief that you are unable to change! Give up being unwilling to change!

Now you're ready to use Worksheet 9 on page 177.

KEEP YOUR LIGHTS ON BY DOING THE FOLLOWING:

1. Recall that the greatest discovery of the 20th century is that you can change and thus alter your circumstances.
2. Remember that the ability to change is your greatest asset.
3. Be assured that great things happen when you embrace new ways of thinking, doing, and learning.
4. Refuse to say, "That's just the way I am."
5. To become good at what you do, be willing to work hard doing it—about 55 hours a week.
6. Continually seek to find a better way in all facets of your life.

WORKSHEET 9
MY GREATEST ASSET

Your greatest asset is your ability and willingness to change. As you accept your greatest asset, think about the following questions and then answer them to the best of your ability today.

1. What are some changes you've made in your life?

____

____

____

____

2. What do these changes tell you about yourself?

____

____

____

____

3. What do you want to change in your life now?

____

____

____

____

4. How will you go about making these changes?

____

____

____

10

Your Recommended Reading List

Many books I've read have richly touched my life, so much so that years ago I made a list of recommended books for my children. That same list now has been changed to "Recommended Books for My Grandchildren." My message to them is simply, "Kids, these books have the potential to change your life, as they have changed mine, always for the better."

I want to encourage you to make such a list for your children and for yourself.

We are not in control of all that happens to us, but we can be in control of what goes into our minds. That control is vitally important for it will contribute to our personal strength and resiliency, while making us more positive, more open, and more caring women and men. Controlling what goes into our minds puts us in charge of where we are going and helps us keep our lights on.

THE VALUE OF BOOKS

Among the gifts most beneficial to me have been books. Sometimes just the inscription from the giver is enough to make my day. One such book came to me from a former business associate who had been promoted in my company. Frankly, I would not have cared what book he had given me because his inscription was more than enough. It read, "Thanks for being my Little Annie."

Only when I read the book did I understand the depth and beauty of that inscription. The book was the story of Annie Sullivan who gave the blind and deaf Helen Keller the gift of communication. Annie Sullivan opened a window for Helen Keller that was to enrich not only her own life but the entire world.

Sometimes I'm sure that the business associate who wrote that inscription was guilty of stretching the truth. But I've always tried to live up to his description. I've tried to be "a little Annie" to those with whom I work, live, and love. His words helped to change my view of myself. Thus, they changed my life.

Another book that profoundly influenced my life was *Fully Human, Fully Alive* by John Powell. His words benefit me each and every day that I live. I quote from that book in each of my seminar presentations. Powell's books and many others help me to better understand myself and others. They help me keep my lights on and become a beacon for others.

MY RECOMMENDED READING LIST FOR MY GRANDCHILDREN

My list of recommended books contains an important message about me. It shows that I have endeavored to fill my mind with information and insights to push me to higher levels. Here are the books that have influenced and continue to influence my life.

1. John Powell, *Fully Human, Fully Alive*
2. John Powell, *Why Am I Afraid to Love?*
3. John Powell, *A Reason to Live and a Reason to Die*
4. Leon Tec, *The Fear of Success*
5. Victor E. Frankl, *Man's Search for Meaning*
6. Paul J. Thomas, *Psychofeedback*
7. Scott Peck, *The Road Less Traveled*
8. Tom Gunnels, *Keep Your Lights On*

   Forgive me, but I just have to add this final book to the list I give my grandchildren! They'll be so proud of their granddad!

YOUR RECOMMENDED READING LIST FOR YOUR LOVED ONES

Having a recommended reading list for your children and grandchildren helps you focus their attention on the importance of reading books. These books have lit the way for you; they can also light the way for those you love.

The list helps you throughout your lifetime for it encourages you to be alert to books that will stretch you intellectually, spiritually, and morally. Such books can enrich all the dimensions of your life. You're ready now to use Worksheet 10. Think about the books that have influenced you. Make a list of them. And, if you choose, share your list with those who are near and dear to you. Remember: your list reveals who you are and what is important to you.

One final word: for your list, choose books that have helped you keep your lights on. Books that have helped you stay focused, encouraged, and enthused!

LETTER FROM "KEEP YOUR LIGHTS ON" SEMINAR

Dear Tom,

I heard you at the Blue Ridge Leadership Conference in the mountains of North Carolina. Thanks for coming through to me loud and clear. June Mize is our local librarian and a member of my balcony. After both of my parents died, she sensed the pain in my life and convinced me to get the help I needed. Her caring about me then and now is one of my richest treasures. One book you recommended (Viktor Frankl's *Man's Search for Meaning*) I bought and lent to a friend. I also found a copy at the library, and Ms. Mize is now reading it. I'm looking now for some of John Powell's books on your recommended list.

Ms. Mize is in my balcony and so are you. Identifying the people in your balcony and reading good books like the ones you recommend are vitally important. "Keep Your Lights On" makes a difference in my life every day.

Bill Chism
personnel manager
Toccoa, Ga.

KEEP YOUR LIGHTS ON BY DOING THE FOLLOWING:

1. Keep a recommended books list to help yourself stay focused, encouraged, and enthused.
2. Consider sharing your list with others. Remember that those you care about most can benefit from what has helped you.
3. Evaluate new books against those already on your list.
4. As you search for good books to read, be aware of how discerning you are becoming about what will enhance your life and the life of those you love.

WORKSHEET 10
MY RECOMMENDED READING LIST

On this page, list the books that are making you who you want to be. Think about the books that have influenced you.

For your list, choose books that have helped you keep your lights on; books that help you stay focused, encouraged, and enthused! Remember: your list reveals who you are and what is important to you.

If you choose, share your list with those who are near and dear to you. Be assured that they can benefit from the books that have helped you become all that you can be.

11

Two Commendation Letters Each Week

Every day, we see or read or hear about people making the world a better place to live. Someone makes an important discovery in science or health care; someone spends seven years writing a novel and it finally gets published; someone wins the Nobel Peace Prize; someone opens a shelter for the homeless.

These people chose to make a difference in the world around them. Their actions touch our lives and make us feel more positive. Thus, they help us realize the potential that lies within each of us.

Of course, every day negativity may jump out at us too. Someone lets us down or gives us poor or indifferent service. Those negatives can color our day and negate our best efforts to be all that we can be.

To counter the effects of negativity and to help myself stay focused on the positive, I have practiced the writing of commendation letters. Each Monday morning when I open my calendar, one of my priorities for the next seven days is to identify two people who merit a letter of commendation. I have practiced this for years, and the results have been phenomenal.

Writing these letters keeps me on the lookout for the positives. And finding the positives worth noting, I am renewed and refreshed to be about my own tasks. In encouraging others, I am most encouraged. And I need all the encouragement I can get! So do we all.

We hunger for approval, for affirmation. When the appropriate circumstances arise, we should freely give this commendation. The payoff for the one who gets the letter is tremendous, but so is the payoff for the letter writer!

If one of our purposes is to be a winner and to encourage other winners, writing commendation letters is one giant step in that direction.

Happenings That Prompt Commendation Letters

Often, when I'm out of town, I'll pick up that city's newspaper. I scan it for stories that suggest a commendation letter. The story might involve the Boy or Girl Scouts, some community work being done by a church group, or some action taken by a citizen or business. I clip the article, put it in my briefcase, and dictate a letter when I get back home. I'm sure that the people to whom I write take pride in getting a commendation letter from someone who was just passing through their town.

My lifelong practice of writing weekly commendation letters has given me many wonderful stories, two of which I want to share with you.

Story #1: When our older daughter was getting married, we had a big wedding. Lots of parties, lots of goings on, relatives coming into town, people staying at our house, receptions being given—the whole litany of events! During that time, we experienced what I have learned to call, in polite circles, a "septic tank crisis." As you can imagine, that problem created a huge damper on the festivities, and my wife, Frankie, gave me the task of taking care of the crisis!

I called the Kington Septic Tank Service. They have a number of trucks in our community designed to handle exactly that kind of problem, and they are radio dispatched promptly. One of their trucks arrived at my home shortly after my frantic plea for help. You can imagine my wife's appreciation for the good results obtained! I was an instant hero. The festivities continued.

Five years later, I was out of town when the "septic tank crisis" occurred again. My wife called the same Kington Septic Tank Service. The dispatcher said she would have one of their trucks there shortly. Frankie started to give our address when the dispatcher said, "Mrs. Gunnels, we know where you live."

Startled, Frankie asked how in the world they could know our address. "Mrs. Gunnels," the dispatcher explained, "We've been in this business for more than 35 years. Do you know how many times we've gotten a commendation letter from one of our customers? The one from your husband is still on the bulletin board."

Story #2: In a career that spanned more than four decades, I regularly commended people within my company. I often got names from our employee publication, which listed people celebrating their five-, 10-, and 15-year anniversaries. To each one I knew, I wrote a short, personal congratulatory letter.

I had no way of knowing how my letters affected those in the company. Then, one day, while one of my agents and I were walking through the halls of our regional office, Alice Carpenter, one of our valued, longtime employees, stopped us in the hall, "Jackson," she addressed the man with me, "you're working for one of the finest men in all the company."

"Wow," I said, turning to Jackson, "If you interrupt that woman, I'm going to hit you in the mouth!"

She continued: "Last night I read every letter this man has written me over the past 35 years. I was reminded again what a fine man he is."

That woman, who was approaching retirement from a responsible position, had saved every letter I had written to her. (I confess that I've also saved all the letters of commendation sent to me over the years.) The prior night, she'd gotten them out and read them again. That she had found them so worthy of saving confirms the value of commendation letters. I give thanks for each one of the letters I have written to her and to others, but at the same time I regret all the opportunities when I might have written letters and didn't.

EXAMPLES OF COMMENDATION LETTERS

What do I say in my commendation letters? Here's a sample of actual letters I've written and mailed.

- To the Garden Plaza Hotel in Murfreesboro, Tennessee:

  Thank you for mailing me the items I left in my room. They arrived on time and I appreciate this added, excellent service.

- To the Indian Oak Inn in Chesterton, Indiana:

  The training level and selection of your people are exceptional and it translates into your guests being exceptionally well treated. I was one of your guests last week and my experience there was made special and enjoyable. At your next employee meeting, I hope you will pass along my commendation.

- To an American Cancer Society worker:

  Congratulations to you on being honored with the American Cancer Society's Lifesaver Award. It is a fitting tribute to the great work you have been doing and no doubt will continue. The example you set encourages all of us to be of greater service to those who need us most. Thanks for your great work.

- To the Utilities Board manager following a major ice storm:

I realize that a lot of your customers had service out longer than the three and one-half days I did and many had service out much less. I just wanted you and all of your associates to know how much we appreciate all their hard work (and sometimes in dangerous circumstances) to restore our power at the earliest possible time. Please let them know of my tremendous admiration for the great work they do for us all.

- To a radio station employee in Knoxville, Tennessee:

Cody, you were a knight in shining armor when you came to our rescue last Friday. My car died of a complete electrical failure in front of Walgreen's. With barely 25 minutes before our plane departed, you came through. Without a moment's hesitation, you rushed us to the airport, luggage and all. Thanks, you've earned my coming-through-award.

- To an insurance company employee:

It is with considerable pleasure that I read of your 40th anniversary. Congratulations on this important milestone and best wishes for your continued good success.

- To our city's mayor:

Your talk at our Downtown Rotary Club was right on target. Your work in behalf of the total community is admirable and much appreciated. We are fortunate to have your leadership skills benefiting us.

- **To a Little League soccer coach:**

  I speak not just for my granddaughter, Lauren, but for all the other young people who have been privileged to benefit from your coaching. They are some very fortunate people because you give of yourself and your energy into that activity. As a very interested and biased grandfather, I wanted to express my personal appreciation and admiration for the good work that you do.

- **To an insurance agent at another company:**

  It was with pride that I read in Sunday's paper the Provident ad commending you for continuing outstanding performance. I am glad to know some of the eagles of this world, and you are one of them. Best wishes always for your continuing good health and success.

- **To a young actor in the stage show *Oliver:***

  Oliver was a smashing success; more so because one of my special friends was in the cast. Michael, the boy with the green pants, was a heartwarming success in a story that was entertaining and appealing. Thanks for helping to make our evening a delightful experience. I hope you'll let me know when you get additional roles.

- **To Jim Clayton, upon his being recognized in the *Forbes* 400:**

  I, too, know cotton picking and tomato-crop tending. Thus, I can and do celebrate when one of us rises to such a plateau of success that he is recognized in the *Forbes* 400. I also applaud your generous support of worthy community causes. You are a victor over your circumstances rather than a victim.

- **To a plastic surgeon who treated my wife following an injury:**

  Thank you for responding so magnificently when I called last week to advise that Frankie had been injured in our home and was being transported to the hospital in an ambulance. I cannot think of a single event where I have earned more points than when I had you there to greet us when she arrived. That meant a great deal to the patient—and equally to her husband. Thanks greatly.

- **To our church sexton:**

  Every time I walk into our church, I am always impressed with how well the property is maintained. I know nothing like this happens by accident. Your close attention to detail enhances our worship and enjoyment of our building's facilities.

> You have earned my appreciation for the excellent way you do your job.

Over the years, I have written and sent hundreds of such letters. I am proud of each letter; my only regret is that I did not write to more people.

I pray that you come to know personally these same feelings for the letters you write and for the letters you may overlook writing. May you know the power of your personal commendations.

YOUR LETTERS OF COMMENDATION

Every day, you see or read or hear about people making a difference. They deserve a note of appreciation. And you can write that note! Don't assume that someone else will write it. The fact is, no one but you can write your commendation.

Your letter does not have to be an epistle. Be assured that a handwritten note can be just as effective as one written on a typewriter or a computer. The form is not nearly as important as the sincerity of your comments.

Make your letter simple, just a few words to express your admiration or appreciation for the work that the person is doing or has done. In writing this letter, you give the person a gift that she or he will treasure. Your letter will generate good will within the person who receives it and within all the people whose lives are influenced by the recipient.

In expressing your commendation, you benefit the most. Why? Because of your own improved view of your world. You find what you look for. Look for good, and you're find it. Commend good, and it will increase and multiply in you and in others.

With all this in mind, complete Worksheet 11 on page 200, and begin to write your commendation letters. Two a week is a great number!

And remember, when possible, to save copies of your letters. Reading them over will help you stay positive about your life and the world around you. Being positive, you can more easily stay focused, encouraged, and enthused. Commendation letters help you keep your lights on!

LETTERS FROM "KEEP YOUR LIGHTS ON" SEMINAR

I now write congratulatory notes each week—making a deposit in people's emotional bank accounts, as Stephen Covey would say. Some weeks I write four or five. The impact on those getting my note is gratifying, but the impact on me is even more amazing. Each letter renews my spirit. Thus, what benefits them also help me—or, again quoting Covey, it's a win-win for all.

Mr. Tim Stanz
Sales Management
Memphis, Tenn.

"Keep Your Lights On" hit home with me. I wrote four commendation letters my first week. When the persons getting my letters get back in touch with me, they thank me for taking the time to be supportive and encouraging. The more I commend and congratulate, the better I feel about me. Thus, I benefit the most. God bless you, and may your lights stay on high beam.

Mr. Michael Selzer
Custom Clothing
Woodmere, Ohio

Many aspects of KYLO impact my life positively. I seek opportunities to send at least two people a commendation letter. This practice not only affirms the people commended, but equally important it improves my focus on finding the positives—and that helps me. This is just one way that KYLO can help us all stay focused and improve our lives.

Andy Womack
State Senator of Tennessee
Nashville, Tenn.

Tom, your idea about writing two commendation letters each week is great. So I decided to write two each day. Finding each day two deserving people for commending is not a problem for me. It is important to keep in touch with friends from your past and present and to be an encourager of youth who are doing something good. Notes of encouragement to staff are important. Dr. Johnson, U.T. president, has a special way of keeping you encouraged by notes he writes. It helps me. My mission statement? I hope they can put on my tombstone, "She made a difference." Tom, I hope you will keep sharing the importance of "keeping your lights on." We all need a little more sunshine.

Joan Cronan
Women's Athletic Director
University of Tennessee

My son Ed and I flew to Anchorage to hear you. Wow! Your suggestion about writing two commendation letters each week is now a part of my habit. The results are astounding. As I help the lights of others shine more brightly; alas, my lights shine more brightly as well.

Dick Randolph
Twice a candidate for
governor of Alaska
Fairbanks, Alaska

KEEP YOUR LIGHTS ON BY DOING THE FOLLOWING:

1. Remember that oral commendations count, but that written commendations count even more.
2. Be assured that two handwritten letters to deserving recipients will change the way you view your world.
3. Do not wait for a history-making event to write.
4. Trust that your letter benefits both the recipient and you.
5. Save a copy of each letter you write; keep each one you receive. Remember that in doing this you increase your dividends and remain positive.

WORKSHEET 11
A LISTING OF THE COMMENDATION LETTERS I WANT TO WRITE

List the names of those who are to receive your first few commendation letters. How will you find those people? Look around you at your family members and friends and peers in the workplace. Read the newspaper. Consider the services that companies provide for you each day and in special circumstances. You have many people to write to. The hard thing is narrowing your list down to two a week!

12

Being Connected to Church and Community

My definition of being connected is very simple: Be involved.

That's it. Our involvement in our place of worship and in our community defines whether we're connected.

Let's begin by considering the following major concept about our personal improvement: When we advance our abilities in any area of our life, we also enhance our abilities in all other areas of our life. When we build a better marriage, we become more effective in our relationships at work. When we improve ourselves professionally, we benefit our home life. That's because we do not live our lives with each role we play being independent. Rather, the parts of our lives are interdependent. Any feeling of success—or failure—in one area flows over to the other areas as well.

Thus, when we stay connected to our place of worship and our community, we enhance and enrich all the other roles we play.

MY INVOLVEMENT WITH MY PLACE OF WORSHIP

My personal involvement in my place of worship has included participation in church management and fund raising. I have also participated in the "ministry of doughnuts"! I began this ministry in 1976. A pastor I know uses my story as one way to encourage members to find their niche. Here's mine and how I found it.

The rector of the church where I worshipped asked me to chair the planning committee for the development of new programs for the adult Sunday School class. As chair, I inherited the task of convening our large adult Sunday School class—250 members. As one of my contributions, I elected to bring doughnuts each Sunday morning.

Thirty minutes before class began, I would be ready with doughnuts displayed and coffee urns filled. As people arrived, I chatted with them and encouraged them to share their thoughts and concerns. Some who came required an extra measure of grace or compassion. Among these were teenagers whose parents were having difficulties or going through a divorce.

Years later I learned how much the doughnuts and conversation meant to those teenagers. As adults, many of them told me that they felt I'd been a caring friend who took a special interest in them. How amazing! Making a difference in someone's life takes as little time and effort as that—providing doughnuts and coffee and a listening ear.

Another of my "ministry of doughnuts" stories involves an elderly lady—Audrey Euhler. She was nearly 80 when I met her at our doughnut-and-coffee table. Her husband had died a few years earlier, and her only son had been tragically killed on the streets of Washington, D.C.

Audrey's personal pain was considerable; some would say she was depressed. She rejected all the attempts that our church members made to include her in their family events. Repeatedly, others told me, "She won't come to your house for dinner. I know, because we've asked her several times."

Audrey became one of my early arriving customers at the doughnut and coffee table. Sometimes there'd be just the two of us for several minutes. At the outset of our conversations, she made it clear that she was not interested in joining anyone for dinner or lunch. "I enjoy being alone" was the way she put it. Still, she was willing to talk and share with me each Sunday, and I tucked away into my memory bank the tidbit about Audrey having been a concert pianist.

As the class convener each Sunday morning, I started including Audrey in my monologue—called the Tom Gunnels' Humor Minute. As I was delivering my humor minute, I'd say, "You know, Audrey just told me a funny story! I want to share it with you."

Audrey would shake her head as a disclaimer, but she seemed to enjoy the attention. Each Sunday, I named Audrey as the source of my humor minute. Gradually, her demeanor began to improve, and she began arriving even earlier for our shared moments over coffee and doughnuts—a good sign that she was beginning to feel open and accepted. She also came to my office a couple of times for advice on insurance and financial matters—other encouraging signs.

One Sunday morning, I said, "Audrey, I need your help. Frankie and I would like to borrow some of your musical expertise. You see, our two daughters are inclined in that area, and we thought that if they played for you, you could advise us if we're on the right track in developing their interests and skills."

Audrey agreed to come to our home to listen to Susan play the piano and Sandra, the violin. She enjoyed the visit and became an encourager for their interest in music. As others learned of her changing attitudes, new invitations went out to her, and she accepted them as well. Finally, she was responding to the love that was reaching out to her.

The story could end right here, but there's more.

Several months later, Audrey was diagnosed with cancer, a fast-acting kind that was to claim her life in a matter of three months. At 82, Audrey faced the end of her life. She had known pain and heartache and tragedy. She had felt so alone that she had, for many years, withdrawn into a shell that prevented anyone from ministering to her needs.

Yet in the month before she died, Audrey confessed to her priest that the last two years of her life had been her best years. The focal point for those two best years, as she described them, was sparked by our church's "ministry of doughnuts." Engaging in conversation over doughnuts and coffee, reaching out to her in humor, recognizing her musical abilities—all this made a difference.

The truth here leapt out at me again—making a difference in someone's life takes so little time!

MY INVOLVEMENT WITH MY COMMUNITY

We can tell similar stories about the importance of your involvement in the community. It matters little about the how you are involved; it matters greatly that you are involved.

During my first wife's long illness, I was active in the P.T.A. It began modestly, when a flyer came home in 1963 asking for volunteers as room mothers for the first and second grades. Our Susan was a first grader and Sue was paralyzed, unable to serve. I became the first dad at Susan's school to become a room mother. Not only did it mean that our daughter had a parent involved in her school, Sue was proud that I was representing her. My sensitivity about being a room mother disappeared when I learned that Susan bragged to one of her classmates, "I have the only dad who is a room mother."

My decision to seek involvement in community work began after hearing University of Tennessee president Andy Holt speak at a chamber of commerce meeting. He emphasized the importance of business people putting back into the community a fair proportion of what they were receiving. He explained eloquently that all of us would be richer, more vibrant, more alive if we sought opportunities to connect to our communities. Being connected, he said, meant being personally involved.

Andy Holt's powerful message was working on my inner self. It was time to "step up to the plate" or write off Holt's appeal. I presented myself at the Knoxville chamber and asked for an assignment. They directed me to their Tourist and Convention Bureau. It turned out that I was the only one in the group who was not in either the restaurant or the lodging industry, businesses that had an obvious interest in promoting conventions and tourism. The next year, 1969, I was elected their president.

Our group's good work rewarded Knoxville with the national convention of the American Bowling Congress, a major plum for a city of our size. That quickly followed by the Hyatt Regency deciding to build a convention hotel in our community, thanks to the combined efforts of the mayor, the chamber overall, and the tourist and convention bureau. At the Hyatt ground-breaking in 1970, several distinguished citizens were on the platform, including then-Senator Al Gore. Keeping everyone's comments brief, including my own, was my major task. It was a big day in Knoxville that helped turn us from a sleepy southern town into a city creating a new vision. In a humorous comment, I told the audience that we had a special agreement with Atlanta, 200 miles south of us: "We will let them have our convention business overflow in exchange for them sending us their excess."

The National Conference of Christians and Jews elected me as president for a two-year term in 1988-90. Working with people of all colors and ethnic backgrounds was an exciting and challenging experience. A high-water mark for me was getting to meet and work with the Rev. W.T. Crutcher, one of America's great preachers and workers in the civil rights movement. He could always see the core issue of any situation and find the compassionate response. When he died toward the end of my term, I was greatly honored to deliver a eulogy at his Mount Olive Baptist Church, one of the largest congregations in Knoxville. Great ministers from all over the United States came to offer tribute to a giant whose compassionate leadership was pivotal in our community as well as the civil rights movement.

During this time, the University of Tennessee appointed the first black head basketball coach of a major school in the south. A university athletic official told the new coach that he would not be accepted for membership at Knoxville's premier country club, the same one where I was also a member. The incident became a major and weeks-long media event. Major stories suggested that the particular country club systematically rejected blacks and Jewish people.

As NCCJ chair, I convened my board. They were people of color and of the Jewish faith. My first item on the agenda was to ask the question, "Considering the controversy of the country club to which I belong, should I resign my membership?"

Remarkably, everyone encouraged me to not resign. "Even if the club is as guilty as they are charged, the last thing we need is people of compassion to not be working within that system," was their central message to me. They earned their stripes in seeking equality of opportunity in every conceivable circumstance, and they gave me an important lesson in leadership: Change is more likely to occur when men and women of good faith work from within rather than from without.

A few months later, I decided to have a golf day for the agents in my district. Two of them were black and I decided to have them as my guests at the same country club. I wondered how the old-time members might interpret this. I did not have long to wait. One of the older members accosted me on a Saturday morning. "Gunnels!" he bellowed out. "I hear you had a couple of black guests play our golf course this week."

"Yes, I did. Tell me," I asked,"how does that make you feel?"

His answer was instantaneous. "I say it was about time for that to happen. Thanks."

YOUR INVOLVEMENT IN CHURCH AND COMMUNITY

Wherever you live and whatever kind of work you do, your place of worship and your community will be far richer if you decide to become involved. Moreover, your involvement will send a message to young people. It will show them how responsible adults act.

You may not be aware that young people—and others too—look to you as a model of how to live life. Because you are an example, whether you want to be or not, you must choose what kind of example you wish to be.

Involvement with your church can help you become the best kind of model for others. When you're involved in your place of worship, you're in contact with better-than-average people.

Of course, a few rascals may attend your place of worship! However, beyond any reasonable doubt, you will be associating, influencing, and being influenced by the better people in your community. Not the most successful necessarily, but those with the higher morals and the greater sensitivity to others and those who are likely the most encouraging.

Associating with these kinds of people is a major stepping-stone in building your path to self-development. In the process, you'll become more sensitive to the needs of others, another worthy building block to a better you.

What can you do at your place of worship? You might teach adults and young people. Or you might use your God-given talents to raise funds, help with administration, host parties for the young and old, call on the sick and homebound, work in a thrift store, serve food to the hungry, greet newcomers, stuff envelopes, cut the grass, paint the classrooms. When you give willingly, God blesses your labor.

Of course, opportunities abound to become involved in your community too. The list of the community organizations with which I've been involved may spark your interest. But you can find many places to use your talents for your community. Simply read your newspaper and you'll discover all sorts of organizations—ones that work with the homeless, the disabled, the ill; ones that provide support for those struggling with abuse; ones that teach an evening class for those seeking help in doing their taxes or buying a home or starting a business. The opportunities are many! As the Christian Gospels say, "Seek and you shall find."

Worksheet 12 on page 212 provides you with the opportunity to consider how you are already involved with your church and community and how you want to become more involved. Remember: What you do is not nearly as important as the doing of it.

As you complete the worksheet, remember, too, that in this book you set nothing down in concrete. You are continually growing and changing. So in the weeks and months ahead, you'll return to many of the worksheets and add new thoughts and realizations. Keep your lights on!

KEEP YOUR LIGHTS ON BY DOING THE FOLLOWING:

1. Remember that any improvement in your interpersonal skills in any aspect of your life automatically spills over to all the other areas as well.
2. Make the conscious decision to be involved at your place of worship and with your community. Call today and announce your availability.
3. Be alert to opportunities to help others who are in a moment of personal crisis.
4. Be ready for the unexpected. Be assured that your gifts will be returned.
5. Be aware that others observe your example and learn from it. Choose the kind of model you want to be for others.

WORKSHEET 12
HOW I STAY CONNECTED TO MY PLACE OF WORSHIP AND TO MY COMMUNITY

To be connected with anyone or with any organization, you need to become involved. On this worksheet, consider how you are involved with your place of worship and with your community.

1. How are you connected to your place of worship? (If you are not connected now, when and how will you be?)

____
____
____
____
____
____
____
____

2. How are you connected to your community? (If you are not connected now, when and how will you be?)

____
____
____
____
____
____
____
____

Getting in Touch with
Your Future

13

Your Personal Contract With Yourself

All of us are in the habit of making contracts. We buy homes, cars, refrigerators, and all sorts of goods and services by signing a contract. The contract specifies who will do what and when. Not only do we expect ourselves to perform according to the contract we sign, but we expect any other parties to the contract to perform as they have agreed to do.

We form corporations; enroll in universities; check into hospitals; buy insurance—all using contracts that specify who will do what and when. Contracts are an integral part of our everyday life, at least insofar as trade and commerce are concerned.

But we have one more contract to put in our portfolio. It may be the most important contract we sign because it is a contract we make with ourselves for our own enrichment. With this contract, we commit ourself to achieve the goals we desire for ourselves for the current year. (We can also make a contract with ourselves for a longer period of time.)

Sometimes we do not achieve the goals we've listed on our contract with ourselves. But this need not discourage us. We can always renegotiate our personal contract in the same way we sometimes renegotiate other contracts.

If we honor all the other contracts in our life, surely we will not do less with the contract we make with ourselves.

MY CONTRACT WITH MYSELF

I have been completing this kind of contract with myself for years. In addition, I've encouraged those with whom I've worked to do likewise. The results have been spectacular.

From 1993 through 1996, I included the following items in my personal contracts.

- **For 1993—**

  Goals: Lose 20 pounds; qualify 10 agents as life leaders club members; establish up-and-running office personnel training programs; personally keep my own lights on.

  Results: Lost 6 pounds; qualified 7 life leaders club members; established the office personnel training programs, which was a huge success; kept my own lights on!

- **For 1994—**

  Goals: Lose 22 pounds by December 31; qualify eight life leaders club members; promote "Keep Your Lights On" presentations; be profitable.

Results: All goals accomplished!

- **For 1995—**

  Goals: Lose 22 pounds; help State Farm make the transition to new agents' agreement; qualify in my district 8 life leaders club members; be profitable in all lines; handle the aftermath of my cancer as a role model.

  Results: Lost 23 pounds; elected to accept retirement at the end of August to start my seminar company—a dramatic change of plans; qualified 7 life leaders club members in my district; remained profitable. Generally, I give myself high marks on the way I have handled the aftermath of my cancer surgery.

- **For 1996—**

  Goals: Lose 12 pounds; complete KYLO manuscript by May 31; market KYLO through chambers of commerce and CEOs; conduct a pilot insurance seminar by July 15.

  Results: Behind schedule on losing weight; renegotiated KYLO manuscript deadline to end of 1996; accomplished the pilot seminar on time; began marketing KYLO through chambers of commerce.

As you can see, one of my goals each year usually involves losing weight. Without that as a conscious goal, there's no telling how much more I would weigh, but it would be considerable!

Following my prostate cancer surgery in November 1994, I discovered anew how much I really like high-calorie foods. In addition to the frustration I experienced with the aftermath of my surgery, I was outgrowing my clothes! So I made a contract with myself to lose 22 pounds in 1995.

I made my contract, duplicated it, and put one copy by my calendar and another by my phone. Every time I looked at my calendar, my contract stared at me! Whenever I reached for the phone, the contract kept its eye on me! I was thus often reminded of what I really wanted to do—lose weight. The final result: I lost 23 pounds.

When I entered 1996, my new personal contract provided that I would lose an additional 12 pounds and that I would complete the manuscript for this book by the end of May. Even though I did not meet that completion date, the contract kept me on my toes and in pursuit of my goals. (When I realized I would not meet the May date, I negotiated a new date—the end of December. And you can see that I met that!)

I confess that I do not always achieve all that I contract with myself to do. But I am absolutely convinced that I get much more done because I make new contracts every year. I consider the practice invaluable for my personal growth and development.

THE 3-STEP PROCESS OF MAKING A CONTRACT WITH YOURSELF

To make your contract with yourself, use Worksheet 13 on pages 223–224 and follow the steps given there and explained below.

Step 1: Select three to five very meaningful goals you want to accomplish in the next 12 months. Select the areas most important to you. Consider personal, health and career achievements as items to include in your contract.

As you make your contract with yourself, include special trips you want to take, books you want to read, educational attainments you want to achieve, performance goals you want to reach.

A word of caution: Be careful what you contract with yourself to do. Make sure that your contract represents what you really want to do because you likely will get everything for which you have contracted.

(You may also want to make a separate contract with yourself on goals you want to achieve over a longer period, say five years.)

Step 2: Sign your contract in front of a witness(es). Ask your spouse, a trusted friend, or a valued coworker to be your witness. When your contract has been properly executed, give a copy to each person who witnessed your signing of it.

What is the value of a friend, or friends, witnessing your contract? Well, there are at least two: (1) By having witnesses, you certify just how significant and important the contract is to you. It is a serious undertaking for you. (2) By giving your witnesses a copy of your contract, you grant them permission to frequently inquire about the progress you are or are not making. During the year, they'll encourage you to do what you have indicated you want to do and already know how to do. Thus, your witnesses become a powerful motivating force for you.

Another word of caution: You don't sign a contract to buy a house you don't really want to buy. Likewise, don't sign a personal contract that you don't expect to honor. Remember: you are both the maker and the makee of this contract.

Step 3: Duplicate your contract. Place one copy with your pocket calendar. Place the other in a clear Lucite holder and put in near your telephone so you will see the contract several times each day. Note that each time you see the contract, it will remind you of the goals you've chosen. This reminder helps you keep your attitudes and actions consistent with the goals you've set.

Be serious about your personal contract, just as you are serious about all the other contracts you make, and you will find that you cannot lose.

Letters from "Keep Your Lights On" Seminar

The "Keep Your Lights On" personal contract gets at the heart of mission-driven decisions without which other factors will influence one's judgment. That contract is vital to illuminate your future (mission) so that you can more clearly see the way to make informed decisions to propel you toward your goals.

Grady Regas, CEO
Quality Development Inc.
Knoxville, Tenn.

My personal contract with me is by far the most important contract I've signed—or sold. It keeps me focused on what I've decided is important to me. Result: I reach more of my goals on time, in spite of distractions. I honor all of the contracts I make—but my personal contract with me is at the top of the list.

Mr. Henry Hooper
Sales
Memphis, Tenn.

KEEP YOUR LIGHTS ON BY DOING THE FOLLOWING:

1. Remember that you have been trained by experience to honor your contracts.
2. Make a personal contract each year with yourself. Contract to achieve the goals you want to achieve for the current year. Consider making a second contract that will include the next five years.
3. Ask one or two people, who are willing to audit your performance, to witness your signing of the contract.
4. Place a copy of your contract by your calendar and by your phone so that you can refer to it at least twice each day.
5. Be assured that your attitudes and actions will tend to match the goals in your contract.

WORKSHEET 13
MY CONTRACT WITH MYSELF

Step 1

I,______________________________, being of a sound, positive mind; committed to the principle of perpetual improvement in all facets of my life; and further accepting the personal responsibility and accountability for who I am, where I am, and where I am going; now therefore do I eagerly execute this contract with myself, promising that I will faithfully accomplish the following goals/tasks by the date noted by each:.

1. ______________________________
2. ______________________________
3. ______________________________
4. ______________________________
5. ______________________________

Step 2

In witness thereof, I sign and date this contract. Entered unto this _____ day of the month of ____________________ of the year _______.

____

Contract Maker/ Date

____

Witness/Date

____

Second Witness/Date

Step 3

I keep a copy of this contract with me at all times, and I read it at least twice each day. Furthermore, I provide a copy of this executed contract to each witness, granting each the responsibility and expectation of inquiring, whenever and wherever, as that person deems prudent, about the progress I am making in fulfilling this contract.

14

The Power of Praise

The most underutilized power on earth is praise. We're talking about using praise every day, several times a day—at home and at work, wherever we are and whatever we do.

One of the great hungers in the world is for more encouragement, more affirmation. None of us has ever gotten too much praise—but many of us have been greatly deprived of affirmations that would have encouraged a more abundant life.

Praise, praise, and more praise are the three essentials of this chapter. The fabulously successful business book *The One Minute Manager* sold in the millions. Its central theme was to "catch people doing things right." We've been trained, the book correctly observed, to catch errors or incorrect actions and to let the errant folks know about their mistakes.

Too many managers and, unfortunately, far too many parents use fear and intimidation as motivational techniques. But this negativity works only for the short term—if it works at all. If we want long-term growth, we must practice the power of praise. We must become a nation of praisers rather than a nation of critics.

And when we do need to give criticism, we must choose to give it lovingly. We must treat others as we want to be treated ourselves. Praise begets growth for when we express appreciation, we encourage further success. Moreover, when we practice praise, we look for the positive in others. Thus, we surround ourselves with the positive rather than the negative. In that way, giving praise helps us grow too. It helps us keep our lights on.

Ideally, we praise others on the spot, on time, and with conviction and enthusiasm. (When appropriate, we add icing on the goodwill cake and follow up with a commendation letter that they will savor time and again! See Chapter 11.)

Since regular praising is such a powerful tool and produces such fantastic results, we need to use it regularly. When we use praise, we multiply our desired results in every area of our life.

Our praise, however, must not be superficial or insincere. Instead, we must regularly and systematically affirm the actions of others as they progress toward desirable goals. When we praise in that way, we promote greater successes. And once we begin to praise others, we find opportunities galore to perfect our art of praising!

PRAISE IN MY LIFE

The people in my balcony were great practitioners of praise. They contributed mightily to my continuing improvement, and I revere them for their contributions to my growth, success, and happiness. Their example taught me to use the power of praise. What they taught me, I learned well for I practice the power of praise often.

Both my daughters became accomplished musicians, one as a pianist and the other as a violinist. My wife, Frankie, and I praised them from the time they first began to show an interest in music. If we had waited for them to make Carnegie Hall, we and they—tragically—would still be waiting, and the world would have less music. We also never asked either daughter to practice her instrument. Instead, we often asked them to play for our enjoyment. A world of difference exists between those two alternatives!

I've always used the power of praise outside my home too. When I became head of an agency unit in 1959, it had about the lowest giving per capita of any group then in the United Way. To elevate our unit to become one of the top givers in our community, I did three things:

- I made sure my own giving set the standard. (The one at the top must always set the example. Anyone who serves as a leader must accept the fact that the role carries a responsibility far beyond the work at hand. An effective leader must lead in every area: delegation, self-discipline, caring, outreach, community support.)

- I communicated to the entire group my own level of giving. Since I would be soliciting the gift of each member of the group, it seemed fair that each should know specifically what my commitment was.
- I complimented each one on his or her generosity. I described each one personally as a generous person. Far from causing anyone to stop at a modest level, the power of that praise prompted each to continue to increase his or her giving level. So much so, that our group earned a deserved reputation for generous support of the United Way.

I have seen people blossom from the power of praise, and so I give it eagerly. But I am blessed because those around me offer praise too.

My own weight reduction program (see Chapter 13) was greatly enhanced by my wife's frequent, daily praise. "Look at my skinny husband," she'd say admiringly as I got dressed each morning.

Now I knew I wasn't skinny—in fact, I'm not now. However, her praise for the progress I was making encouraged me to continue to earn that praise by continuing the progress. Great things happen when we hold true to the course we set. Her praise kept me counting the calories and making good choices regarding the food I ate.

USING YOUR POWER OF PRAISE

Simply stated, you must praise not just what you see today, but what you want to see in the future. Read that sentence again. Then reread it!

Learning to praise the qualities you want to see in others before you see these qualities will produce huge dividends. And wonder of wonders, praise works as well at home as it does in business, in our place of worship, and throughout our community. Your praise encourages others to continue to improve.

Don't wait for the completed miracle. Just see genuine—I did not say dramatic—progress and use praise. Practice until praising others becomes second nature to you. A simple, "Good job, Frank (or whomever)" is a great way to get started. Go on from there. You'll quickly become an artist at praise.

And using praise helps you stay focused and encouraged and enthused. Why? Because you're looking for the positive.

Now you're ready to use Worksheet 14 on page 232 to list all the people you want to praise.

LETTERS FROM "KEEP YOUR LIGHTS ON" SEMINAR

Since I heard your "Keep Your Lights On," I've taken a different tack. I write praise letters. I became involved in promoting the organ donor program. I've gotten to know some people who desperately needed an organ transplant and—fortunately—got one. I'm careful to praise the ones making the gift possible, praise the one getting the new organ, and encourage everyone not to bury their organs with them. A friend's wife recently got a lung transplant, and it has been a miracle. Now her lights are shining.

Tom Clark
Insurance Sales
La Vergne, Tenn.

Your "Keep Your Lights On" message opened a new concept with me: I now realize that I have a balcony of people supporting me. I had not stopped to think about it, but you brought them to mind. It was invigorating. They helped me because they saw something special in me and that is a wonderful feeling. I've paraphrased your talk several times with my unit. The results have been very upbeat, positive. Whatever we can do to help others keep their focus, their encouragement, and their enthusiasm—that is what I want to do.

Terrence Bailey
Insurance Sales
Louisville, Ky.

KEEP YOUR LIGHTS ON BY DOING THE FOLLOWING:

1. Embrace the belief that praise is a powerful tool for helping others and that it is the most underutilized power you have.
2. Praise not just what you see, but what you want to see.
3. Start your praising when progress is made. Don't wait until the person reaches his or her goal. Accept that holding back your praise is a way of being stingy.
4. Remember: be a continual praiser not a constant critic.
5. When criticism is necessary, do it lovingly.

WORKSHEET 14
THE POWER OF MY PRAISE

List examples of how you plan to use the power of praise. As you do this, be aware that you're moving toward some important understandings of who you are and what you are all about.

Remember: Praising others keeps you positive. Looking for actions to praise, keeps you looking for the good in people and in the world around you. That helps you keep your lights on. Dwell in positivity, not negativity!

15

Your Own Ralph Waldo Emerson Club

More than 100 years ago, Ralph Waldo Emerson, one of America's great thinkers, made the following profound statement: "What I most need is someone or something to get me to do what I already know how to do and what I've already said I wanted to do." What a stunning, insightful realization!

All of us are like Emerson: we need someone or something to get us to do what we already know how to do and what we've already said we wanted to do. Most of us, however, are our own worst enemy. Nobody holds us back the way we do.

Given our tendency to remain irresolute and to think ill of ourselves, Emerson's statement can add light to our paths and help us come closer to all that God designed us to be and all that we want to be. And that's why we need to be in a Ralph Waldo Emerson Club!

This club should be at the top of our listing of all the activities we might initiate to promote our success and that of others. Why? Because first and foremost, it's successful; it works. Second, it costs only the time involved. Further, all of us who are members truly enjoy one another's company. We have fun together.

But most of all, all of us in a Ralph Waldo Emerson Club get more done when we benefit from the unconditional support and encouragement of fellow travelers along the road to excellence.

What Is a Ralph Waldo Emerson Club?

The Ralph Waldo Emerson Club serves as an informal board of directors for each of us who are members. We offer suggestions, ideas, and encouragement to one another. We also hold each other responsible for doing what we have agreed to do.

In a Ralph Waldo Emerson Club, we share our personal vision with the other members; we establish and share our individual plans to achieve that vision; and we report periodically to each other on what we are doing, what we want to do, and what we will do to accomplish our goal.

Such a club encourages us and holds us accountable to do what we want to do and what we can do. Each of us in the club agrees to be open with every other club member and to share his or her best ideas in a spirit of cooperation and helpfulness. In this way, we prove the axiom that several heads are better than one.

Any group of people can form a Ralph Waldo Emerson Club. Students may choose to form such a club to hold themselves accountable for study disciplines. Parents may help one another maintain enthusiasm and encouragement as they strive to parent well. They may also share ideas about how to accomplish such a task in a difficult world. Professionals from several walks of life may join together to share their personal ambitions and their plans for reaching those ambitions in a suitable time frame.

WHAT'S A RALPH WALDO EMERSON CLUB LIKE?

The ideal number of members in one club is about six to eight. When a particular club gets too many members, say 10 or so, then the club should break into two halves to form two new clubs. Participants in an Emerson club should include only those who really want each member to succeed at his or her stated goal.

Ideally, the club members meet weekly. (They should always meet at least once a month.) They can meet for breakfast, over lunch or dinner, over dessert, or simply over a cup of coffee. They have a definite starting and ending time, a specific date and time of the month. (For instance, each Monday for lunch at a specified restaurant, from 12:00 to 1:15.) Someone keeps minutes so that each person's plans become a matter of record.

Usually, each club has a central focus: career, personal development, parenting, marriage, students, Bible study, and so on. (Often, because of their varied interests and roles, people belong to more than one Emerson club.) The members of each club commit themselves to share plans and ideas to help one another. Members also agree to respect one's another's need for confidentiality.

Some businesses have a Ralph Waldo Emerson Club to help employees remain steadfast to their goals and that of the company. However, not all members in such a club benefit equally. Why? Because such a group is not voluntary and so some members may not have the enthusiasm and desire for achievement that others have.

Ralph Waldo Emerson Clubs succeed best when members come together voluntarily and are willing to share and to be held accountable for what they say they are going to do.

START YOUR OWN CLUB

There is tremendous power in a club in which you are open with the other members and in which you offer your best ideas to fellow members to help them on their journey. Moreover, the positive benefits from having others invest their time and energies in your success is spectacular, helping to keep you on target.

The power of such a group can be awesome. But let me give you a word of caution: Don't become involved in one unless you are serious about rising to the top! The ideas and encouragement of the club members will be so prolific they will amaze you.

The club cheers you on and helps you access your own power. Once you've formed a club, you'll wonder how in the world you ever got along without the help of the other members. (Answer: Not nearly as well!)

As you fill out Worksheet 15 on page 238, remember Ralph Waldo Emerson's words: "What I most need is someone or something to get me to do what I already know how to do and what I've already said I wanted to do." Find people who will get you to do what you already know how to do and what you've said you want to do. Those people will help you stay positive and keep your lights on!

KEEP YOUR LIGHTS ON BY DOING THE FOLLOWING:

1. Begin your Ralph Waldo Emerson Club by forming around some common denominator, such as parents, students, supervisors, people in business with a common vision.
2. Meet regularly, preferably weekly, but in no case less than once a month.
3. Invite each person to share openly his or her ambitions, goals, problems, and doubts and to draw on the strength of the entire group for encouragement, ideas, solutions—whatever is needed to get the task done.
4. Keep minutes so that the members can note their progress.

WORKSHEET 15
MY RALPH WALDO EMERSON CLUB

Decide what common denominator you want as the linchpin for the organization of your Ralph Waldo Emerson Club. Then list the names of those people whom you want to invite to join the club. Write down the date when you will contact each one.

The Rules for the
Journey

16

The Rules for Keeping Your Lights On

"Tell me the rules, and I can plan any game." That's a typical statement for many business people striving for success. Moreover, those of us trying to become more ourselves and to live a good life sometimes make this statement too.

First, we have to know this—life is not a game. It's serious business. It's the real thing, and when the final bell rings, that's it. No instant replays; no second chances. If we miss, we miss.

In this book, I've shared a lot about me and how I live my life. The stories I've told carry messages about my beliefs. Some of them I've stated boldly. Others, I've hinted at. Now I'd like to share in a succinct manner the guidelines, the rules, that have helped me keep my lights on.

All of us have rules for driving, for building a house, for playing any sport. We know that we perform better in any activity if we know and follow the rules. Here are the rules that will help you journey to become all God meant you to be.

THE SEVEN RULES FOR THE JOURNEY

I've been able to come up with seven rules for living my life. They help me each day to stay focused, encouraged, and enthused.

Rule 1: Remember that you are in charge.

No longer can you make someone else responsible for who you are or for where you're going. Whatever you're going to do, you're the one who's going to do it.

Even though I've said that life isn't a game, I'm going to use a game metaphor with this rule because so many of us understand sports and the implications of playing to the best of our ability. And so I'm saying that now's the time to step to the bat and be responsible for your own hits and misses. There's no designated hitter for you; you have to take your own turn at bat.

You're the one who can hit the runner in or hit the homerun over the left-field fence. No one else can do it for you. Not your boss, not the economy, not the politics of the moment, not chance, not good luck, not your spouse—no one but you.

When you consider your life, would you have it any other way? Would you willingly let someone else take charge of your life? I suspect not.

Rule 2: Never think of yourself as a victim.

Victims, by their very status, aren't responsible for who they are or where they are. Every time you treat yourself as a victim, you tell yourself—quietly, silently, subconsciously—that the events and circumstances surrounding you are beyond your control. But if life is beyond your control, then you can do nothing to change your circumstances. Thus, you become a loser.

Victimhood implies failure, both to those individuals who see themselves as victims and to others who are likely to see such an example as validating the worst part of themselves. Victims do not belong in the world of doers.

For years, many programs in the daytime TV industry have built their programming around the honoring of victims. That's been a tragic mistake. Society becomes healthy only when it honors victors. Why? For two reasons: Because such honor encourages the victors in their quests and because it provides all of us with examples from whom we can draw strength.

Rule 3: Start now.

Begin your journey to keep your light on now—not tomorrow, not even later today, but now. You doom your program of continuous self-improvement when you say, "Oh, I'll start tomorrow. Next week. Next year." You need to start now because if you don't, you probably won't start at all. The road to you-know-where is paved by procrastinators.

Rule 4: Believe that the best is ahead of you, not behind.

Grab hold of this rule and believe in it. If you don't, you deny yourself the opportunity to grow. For as long as your life and health permit, keep always in front of you the belief that your best is yet to be. Recognize your "mountaintops" as opportunities for new growth.

Rule 5: Give up no dream until you have a better one to take its place.

This rule may sound simple, but it's truly difficult. People often set out on a direction and then, facing some discouragement, abandon that course without setting a new one. You may have done this yourself.

Hold on to your dreams of possibilities because not only do they give purpose and direction to your life, they also define who you are. Who you are matters greatly. Keep your dream in the forefront as a compass for your journey. Dream great dreams! Realize your possibilities!

Rule 6: Celebrate often.

Regularly commemorate your progress toward a new level of achievement. In these joyful moments, you offer yourself—and others—encouragement for the tasks ahead. When you wait until reaching a goal before celebrating, you deny yourself the energy producing feedback that will help you persist.

Most individuals and most organizations do not know when and what to celebrate. So celebrate early and often. The celebrating affirms you and your dreams and sustains you on the journey. Celebrating helps you stay the course.

Rule 7: Always be selling.

Wherever and whenever, you are selling, making impressions, extolling your ideas, seeking new opportunities. But the most important sale you make each day happens the first thing every morning when you arise and proclaim that this is the "day that the Lord has made."

One of my grandsons, when he was three, would open the curtains when he got out of bed each morning and proclaim, "Another great day." It did not matter if it was snowing or raining or if the sun was shining, it was "another great day."

Be like that small child, get a fresh beginning each day by first selling yourself on you, on your opportunities, and on your talents. You're on the road to a great day when you start it off by proclaiming it.

Four Basic Truths That Help You Live the Rules

I'd like to also share with you four basic truths that seem almost self-evident when we think about what makes us feel focused, encouraged, and enthused. These truths help you live the seven rules I've detailed in this chapter. When you have your lights on, you live these truths.

- You encourage yourself when you encourage others.
- You enhance your own enthusiasm when you help enthuse someone else.
- You cannot give to others anything that you have not claimed for yourself.
- You cannot earn a dividend on an investment you have not made.

Recently I saw the following definition: "Insanity is continuing to do the same thing and still expecting better results." In this world such insanity is . . . insane.

Don't continue to do the same thing and expect better results. Resolve to try something new and get those better results!

Now you're ready to make the biggest change in your life!

SOME FINAL THOUGHTS FOR YOU

Only when you have absorbed these four truths can you follow the seven rules of this chapter. Together, these basic truths and rules will enrich your life. So live life with all your heart. Now! Today!

Make your life count. Leave nothing to chance. Don't be like those people who spend more time and imagination planning a family vacation than they do in mapping out what they will be doing with their opportunities for the rest of their lives. Don't treat life casually if you want to become fully who you are.

And I believe that you do want to become a person who keeps your lights on, who stays focused and encouraged and enthused. How do I know? Because you've read this far in the book! You're excited about the possibilities of discovering more in you than you ever thought possible. You feel good about yourself. Well, stay that way! Remember: your performance increases as you begin to value yourself and all your abilities, gifts, and opportunities!

Worksheet 16 on pages 249–251 will help you apply the seven rules of this chapter to your life. Note that the worksheet provides space for you to add new rules to your list. In adding new rules, always choose ones that contribute to your becoming who you really want to be for yourself and for all those who look to you as a model of how to live a full and fulfilling life.

Keep your lights on!

Letter from "Keep Your Lights On" Seminar

Your "Keep Your Lights On" presentation is in my memory and in my heart. We all have mountains to climb as we move toward God's plan in our lives. We need to continue to keep our eyes on our goal and the lights that others—like you—shine for us.

Lisa Elias
Insurance and financial products
Memphis, Tenn.

Thank you for your inspirational words and the vulnerability and humility that came through in your presentation. It was a privilege to spend some time with you one-on-one. Thank you for touching my heart.

Dennis C. Warren
Woodinville, Wash.

KEEP YOUR LIGHTS ON BY DOING THE FOLLOWING:

1. Know your rules and follow them.
2. Hold on to the seven basic rules:

    Remember that you are in charge.

    Never think of yourself as a victim.

    Start now.

    Believe that the best is ahead of you, not behind.

    Give up no dream until you have a better one to take its place.

    Celebrate often.

    Always be selling.
3. Encourage yourself by encouraging others.
4. To become more enthused, enthuse others.
5. Remember that you cannot give to others what you have not claimed for yourself.
6. Earn dividends by making an investment in life.
7. Consciously and intentionally keep your lights on.

WORKSHEET 16
MY RULES FOR KEEPING MY LIGHTS ON

Remember that knowing a rule is not enough. You have to own the rules adopt it, believe in it, live it.

That's the purpose of this worksheet, which repeats the seven rules from Chapter 16. What you need to do is affirm your adoption of each one. Only then does the rule becomes yours. So affirm each one, and if you wish, add your comments.

You may also want to add other rules. Just be sure that they contribute to your growth as a person. What kind of person do you want to be? You want to become wholly yourself, the person God designed you to be. Why? Because this will mean peace and happiness and growth for you and for all those who look to see how you live your life.

1. I affirm the following rules:

   Rule 1: I am in charge of who I am and where I am going.

   Rule 2: I am not a victim. I can't be when I am in charge.

   Rule 3: I am starting today on my "Keep Your Lights On" journey.

   Rule 4: My best is not behind me, it is still ahead of me.

   Rule 5: I will not relinquish any dream until I have a bigger one to take its place.

   Rule 6: I will often celebrate my progress.

<u>Rule 7</u>: I will always be selling myself—and others—through affirmations.

2. To the list above I add the following rules and understandings:

____

____

____

3. Now I affirm for myself these five basic truths:
   - I know that when I encourage others I will also be encouraging myself.
   - I know that when I help others maintain their enthusiasm I will better maintain my own.
   - I cannot give to others anything that I have not first claimed for myself.
   - I cannot earn a dividend on an investment I have not made.

4. Now I affirm the following skills and talents, which I claim for myself.

____

____

____

5. Now I affirm the following opportunities, which life is presenting to me.

____

____

____

6. Having reviewed my answers, I now affirm the following action, which I choose to take.

____

____

____

____

____

____

Signature and date

Post Word

Having felt the message of *Keep Your Lights On* in your heart, you're on your way to becoming who God meant you to be. Don't think otherwise. Great things happen in your life when you stay the course with graciousness and with a belief that all is possible when you choose to stay focused, encouraged, and enthused. When you keep your God-given lights on, you become a beacon for others. Then you light the world!

Long before I formulated the ideas outlined in this book, I came to realize that all of us get up in the mornings, sometimes when we don't feel like it. We face the day when the day is not at all promising. All of us do a lot of things a lot of times that we don't feel like doing. The fact is that all of us who become good and productive parents; spouses; workers in our place of worship, community, and job; and good and productive and responsible and accountable people know that often we do things that we don't feel like doing and don't enjoy doing. Still, each of us must do what must be done.

Often I've reminded young people—and others as well—that if they only do what they feel like doing, they're not going to get much done. Each of us has a mountain to climb. The truth is that we'll climb our mountain only to the extent that we're willing to tackle the task regularly and systematically—and not just when the fancy strikes us.

One of the things that helps me do even those things that may not appeal in the beginning is the realization that others are looking to me for enlightenment. This realization encourages me to stay positive. I know that many people look to me as an example of how to live life fully, of how to be all that they can be.

That responsibility is awesome. Of course, I often fall short in fulfilling it. But that does not negate one bit the face that being a beacon for others *is* my responsibility.

When I falter, I quickly get back up and tackle my task with renewed determination. How am I able to do this? Because of my commitment to keeping my lights on.

And so I leave you with three final thoughts:

- Remember that keeping your lights on is an intention, a stated objective, a personal goal. Because it is so, you usually realize when your lights are off. When this happens, quickly go about the job of getting them back on.

- Trust me: the more you do what you do not want to do, the more inclined you are to enjoy doing just that.
- When your lights are off, as they will sometimes be, always seek the counsel of someone whose lights are obviously shining brightly. If you seek the solace of those whose lights are dimmed, you perpetuate your own darkness.

The British have a phrase I'll borrow now: "There you have it." To which I will add, "Keep climbing your mountains. As you climb, make use of *Keep Your Lights On*. It will help you in the climbing."

When our paths cross, I trust I'll know you by the brightness of your lights—and you'll recognize me in the same way. I pray that all of us will be ambassadors of light; that all of will keep our lights on and be beacons to light the path for others. In this way, we live our lives for the good of the universe!

W9-AVN-764

2013

The Duke of Morrison Street

A Leopold Larson Mystery

Copyright 2009 Orrin Onken
First Printing
All Rights Reserved
Published by Salish Ponds Press, LLC
editor@salishpondspress.com
ISBN-13 978-0-9824564-0-8
ISBN-10 0-9824564-0-9
www.salishpondspress.com
LCCN 2009908350

The Duke of Morrison Street

A Leopold Larson Mystery

By
Orrin Onken

Salish Ponds Press LLC
Fairview, Oregon

To Margo

Chapter 1

I spent every Sunday afternoon for fifteen years doing the New York Times crossword puzzle on the bar at Hal's Place. Hal's was a dive that served liquor to inner city alcoholics. Hal's knew its place in the world. No pool tables, no little wienies from a jar, no video poker. Just cheap strong drinks. Hal's Place was a service to the community. Drunks, drug addicts, hookers, and small time criminals could meet at Hal's, make a deal, find a mate for the night, and drink. People smoked cigarettes and told each other lies. People shot dope in the bathrooms. Hal, a somber gray Santa Claus of a man, presided over it all from his stool by the register. They said he had a forty-five caliber pistol and a baseball bat under the counter. I never saw either one, but I believed they were there.

Winter had come full force to Portland and the rain had begun in earnest. Everything was wet. The incessant drizzle fed a moss that climbed up the walls of buildings and turned the sidewalks pale green. It hung in tendrils from telephone wires and would grow up a man's leg if he stood in one place too long. The wet cold made my fifty-year-old joints ache.

I pushed my empty glass forward to let Hal know I wanted another shot of soda water. He slid off his stool and waddled down the bar. I watched his hands as he filled my glass. His tattoos had turned the color of bruises.

"Leo," he said, "I told a guy you would be here today."

"Who?"

"A guy I know. A biker. He needs a lawyer."

"I can't keep people out of jail, Hal. I'm a probate lawyer. I do wills and shit like that."

"I know what kind of law you do," Hal said, "You think everybody I know is a criminal?"

"That's exactly what I think," I said. He snorted and shuffled off to his stool.

On that rainy Sunday I had been off the booze for a little over three years. Certain irregularities involving client funds had cost me a five year suspension from the practice of law. I drank my way through the suspension driving forklift, then checked myself into rehab. To get the license back I had to complete rehab, cut out the booze, and go to meetings of Alcoholics Anonymous. It was the price of being allowed to practice again. Nothing in the deal said I had to quit doing crosswords at Hal's.

Back in the law business, I waded into the world of wills, trusts and discontented heirs. The idea came from a Mormon mortician I met in rehab. When I met him, he'd been kicked out of his profession, kicked out of his marriage and kicked out of his church. In between watching *Days of Wine and Roses* and going to counseling sessions, the two of us schemed ways to make money when we got out. He figured to do low-budget cremations and send the family legal work my way for a modest kickback. I didn't know much about probate at the time, but lawyering ain't rocket science. Doing law for dead people sounded like a quiet practice. No criminals with a nasty tendency to hold a grudge if you didn't win their cases. No fighting over who had to take care of somebody's snotty kids.

I never heard from the Mormon again after getting

out of treatment, but with rehab behind me and license in hand the probate thing still seemed like a good idea. When sober I could make a living doing most any kind of law. The day the Oregon State Bar handed me my ticket back, all I wanted was a safe little office gig doing something that would leave me a few bucks at the end of the month.

"What's this friend of yours want?" I asked.

"Something to do with his old lady," Hal said. "Her father died and she thinks she's entitled."

"They got any money?"

"Can't say for sure, but I don't think this guy would be asking about a lawyer if he couldn't pay." That was a good sign. Most people looking for a lawyer in a place like Hal's were on the scam for freebies. No matter how uneducated, every drunk knows enough Latin to say *pro bono*.

"This guy got a name?" I asked.

"Churley. Churley Dowd."

"Never heard of him," I said.

I kept coming back to law because, when it comes right down to it, the work is easy. I knew from earning a living during my suspensions that painters, fork lift drivers, taxi drivers, and just about everybody works harder than lawyers, but lawyers get paid more. Lawyers don't make money like, movie stars, professional athletes, or dentists, but everything considered, lawyers get paid well enough. Maybe we live in a litigious culture. Maybe lawyers grease the wheels of justice. I couldn't care less. I am a lazy man, and practicing law is the only way I know how to make a living sitting in a chair.

The first time I saw Churley Dowd he was soaked. He came through the door of Hal's and stood inside letting the rain drip off his leathers onto the floor. The Oregon rains are not kind to motorcycle riders. Churley was a small thin man who even in boots had to stand straight to reach five foot two. He was normal, not a midget or a dwarf, just small.

He took off his wet jacket and laid it on a table by the door. The emblem on the back said "Rebellion Dogs" and had a graphic of a pit bull. The motto at the bottom was "Clean and Sober." He looked at Hal, and Hal nodded toward me.

"Coke please," he said, and took a seat on the stool next to me. Hal popped the tab on a Coke can and set it in front of him. Looking at me, the biker asked, "Are you the lawyer?"

"I'm a lawyer," I said, "Leo Larson."

"Churley Dowd." He stuck out his hand. "I'm pleased to meet you, Leo."

I gave his hand a shake. It was wet from the rain. "Yeah. Same here," I said.

"What kind of law do you practice?"

"Little of this, little of that. Wills and trusts mostly. What do you need?" Churley took a drink of his Coke. He had the stained hands of someone who works with motors.

"Anything else? Criminal defense? Personal injury?"

"Nope. Just probate. I represent the dead, the nearly dead, and their greedy relatives."

What I told him wasn't strictly true. After law school, when I had a lot more energy, I did criminal defense and learned that I didn't like criminals. My criminal clients were all whiners with some complaint against the world that they just couldn't get over. With the exception of drug dealers, I hated all my criminal clients. I didn't like the drug dealers much better, but the drug dealers didn't whine, didn't claim they were innocent, and didn't ask for credit. They put cash on the desk and asked only that I do my best. The rest of my criminal clients wanted miracles on a payment plan. After a couple years I was doing all drug dealers, a business that might have worked if I hadn't started taking a lot of fees out in product. My association with drug dealers led to my first suspension and my first trip to rehab.

"Do you help people get inheritances?" Churley asked.

"Yeah, I do," I said.

"How long have you been doing that kind of law?"

"Churley, if there is any cross-examining to be done here, I'd like to be the one doing it."

After dumping criminal law, criminals, and criminality in general, I did what every shingle-hanging lawyer does: personal injury. Doing personal injury law has the same combination of tedium and excitement as playing slot machines. You watch different combinations of the same mind numbing pattern hoping for the fates to grant you that one perfect alignment of facts, law, and insurance coverage that will make you rich. You spend your days listening to stories about how some sad bastard will have to spend twenty years in chiropractic care because there was a broken bottle of ketchup in the middle of the aisle at Safeway. You pay the office rent taking thirty percent of a lot of nickel-and-dime whiplash cases while waiting for the big one. Like addicts dreaming about the big heroin score, personal injury lawyers dream of that one verdict which will pay off the debts and buy a vacation house at the beach. For me and a lot of other lawyers that case never arrived.

I hung in with personal injury for seven years, hating every minute. Then came the problems with the trust account which led to the aforementioned five year suspension and another trip to rehab. Five years was the most they were allowed to dish out. The next time it would be disbarment.

"I'm sorry," Churley said. "I am not trying to be rude. My wife needs a lawyer who knows about inheritances and Hal said you did that kind of thing. I respect Hal and don't mind taking his advice. On the other hand, seeing a lawyer in a place like this does not instill me with confidence." Although oblivious to the ridiculousness of his appearance, the diminutive biker was not as dumb or roughly hewn as I had expected.

"I suppose not," I said.

Churley took another drag on his Coke and eyed my drink. "You a friend of Bill's?" he asked. The question was an insider's way of asking whether I was a member of Alcoholics Anonymous. I hated the question.

"Yeah. I'm a friend of Bill's," I said.

"Me too."

"I figured that. I saw the jacket."

"How long have you been clean?" he asked.

"Three years."

"That's good," he said. "My wife's name is Daisy. Her father died in January of this year. She is pretty sure she should inherit something, but doesn't know how to go about things."

I put one of my business cards on the table. "Have her call me to set up an appointment."

"She didn't take my name when we got married.

Her name is Twill. Daisy Twill."

"I'll remember."

I figured nothing would come of it. People you meet in bars don't call. I watched Churley Dowd put on his wet leathers and head back into the rain. I knew his wife. I hadn't really met her, but I'd spent some time in the same room with her, and once you've been in the same room with Daisy Twill you never forget her.

I rented my office in the Villanova Building in February of 2002, the same month my reinstated license took effect. My landlord was a divorce lawyer who leased the extra offices in his building to lawyers, accountants, and insurance salesmen. The directory by the front door listed me as "Leopold Larson, Attorney at Law."

The Villanova Building was a stone's throw from auto row in a commercial neighborhood known for car lots, gypsies, hookers and cheap rents. My office window looked out on the back lot of Mel's Patriotic Used Cars where there was no credit check for vets. The squat gray Villanova Building housed eight small offices arranged on either side of an unheated hallway. The building always had a vacancy, and the sign visible from the street had a permanent neon announcement of space for rent. The owner of this white collar tenement and occupier of two of the offices was Torkum Masoogian

Torkum Masoogian stood five foot eight and tipped the scales at over three hundred and fifty pounds. Balding, with a gray comb-over that levitated about an inch above his shiny bald head, he ran "Torkum Masoogian and Associates." The phrase "and Associates" in a law firm name usually means the named member is an egomaniacal asshole who imagines himself a firm, but in reality employs a series of timid, beaten lawyers willing to accept a regular salary in return for doing the actual work in the office and putting up with the owner's abuse. Or at least that's how it worked with Torkum. The sad part was that in a different time and in a different building I'd been the associate of Torkum Masoogian and Associates. So when it came time to hang out my shingle and try the probate thing, it was as natural as rain in Portland for me to look him up.

Torkum made most of his money from being a landlord, but he also ran a moderately successful divorce shop. His shtick was a regular ad in the newspaper announcing, "Divorce Attorney For Women Only." The implication of the ad was that Torkum had some special skill or special sympathy for women in divorce. The truth was that he was a misogynist who'd found women less adept than men at uncovering his incompetence.

Of all the crappy lawyers I'd met over the years, Torkum was the worst. If he ever got the law right in one of his cases it was because his associate had done the work. But when he got a whiff of money, Torkum was tenacious. He clamped on to his cases and never let go. Other lawyers backed off, gave up, abandoned their clients and left the profession—anything—just to get out of a case with Torkum on the other side. He was the kind of man who made other people think *life is too short for this.*

When I walked into Torkum's building in 2002 to ask about a place to rent, he was typing in the reception area. He had wedged his flabby butt onto a wheeled steno chair like Bob Dylan's mattress on a bottle of wine. He always maintained a secretarial station at the front of his office and used it a lot, but hadn't had a paid secretary since Peggi Iverson, ten years earlier.

"Four hundred dollars a month. First and last up front," he said.

"Nice to see you too, Torkum, after all this time." I stepped up to the counter that separated the small waiting room from the secretarial space.

"I heard you got your ticket back. What are you going to do this time?"

"Probate. Guardianships and conservatorships. Old people law," I said. He stood and waddled across the reception area. The steno chair stayed put proving that it had not been up his ass. Torkum took keys from a drawer and tossed them to me.

"Office 106," he said. "That will be eight hundred bucks." I counted out eight one hundred dollar bills onto the counter, took the keys, and walked down the hall to the office of Leopold Larson. I was in the law business again.

The nice thing about the law is that it doesn't require much start up capital. You pony up for bar dues and you are a phone, word processor, and case of copy paper away from being a professional. I'd managed my forays into and out of the profession with two valuable tools. The first was a long term lease on a ten-by-twenty storage space at Donnelli's Mini-storage where I kept everything from the staple removers to my yellowing college degrees. The second was Peggi Iverson.

Peggi Iverson was the finest legal secretary, receptionist, paralegal, and all purpose assistant in Portland. I met Peggi when we were both working under the miserable fat thumb of Torkum Masoogian. We both quit Torkum's office on the same day. I quit because he was a miserable fat fuck. She quit, I think, because he tried to stick his hand down her pants. And thus, we ended up together. Peggi had no training, no education, and no social skills. What she did possess, however, was that steel-cold loyalty, born and bred in trailer parks and rent-by-the-week motels, that motivates certain women to stay with lazy drunken men in the face of all adversity and logic. At home in the backstreets of the Heartland Mobile Estates she had given birth to two children by two different fathers. These two criminals in training were the love of her non-working life. When I had work, she was the only other person I would ever allow in my office. Law is a business where, for good reason, members of the staff loathe their bosses. Much evil comes from that. Peggi Iverson kept the evil away from me.

As far as I could tell, Peggi's stout pear-shaped body was completely covered with freckles. In idle moments I had pondered the question of whether her wide butt, the bulwark of her pear shape, was as freckled as her face. Having seen her angry response to Torkum's sexual advances I was careful to stay away from any physical exploration that would have answered the freckle-butt question. That did not mean, however, I wasn't interested. On several occasions over the years she had inadvertently leaned over in a way that allowed me to see a fully freckled breast. She had no more breast than you would find on an obese man, but what she had was covered in freckles.

Peggi lived in a mobile home at the end of Lonely Street. Lonely Street wasn't an official Portland street, but rather the name of the single road that ran down the middle of the Heartland Mobile Estates, so named because the previous owner had been a bi-polar Elvis fan before he killed himself. Down at the end of Lonely Street, Peggi raised her two children and gossiped across the fence with the kind of men who wear mullets and know how to fix Camaros.

After renting the office from Torkum, I called Peggi. In the past I'd done a little free work for the folks on Lonely Street and had a few favors I could call in. When Peggi put out the word the pickups rolled and in no time the desks, computers, pictures, and other lawyer's tools disappeared from the wet caverns of Donnelli's Mini-storage into office number 106 in the Villanova Building. Peggi, who had been directing traffic at the airport in my absence from the profession, put away her reflective yellow vest and took out her good white blouses. Several years earlier she'd made herself a name tag that said, "Peggi Iverson, Legal Assistant." She took the tag from her jewelry box, affixed it to a pressed blouse, and once again had more than just a job. At the Heartland Mobile Estates, being able to earn a living sitting in a chair was testimony that you had intelligence above that of the common mob.

While Peggi worked on her phone persona talking to the dial tone—"Office of Leopold Larson, may I help you?" "Leopold Larson's office, may I be of assistance." "Leopold Larson, Attorney at Law."—I set about becoming a probate lawyer. When I first fired up the computer at the Villanova building all I knew about probate was what I'd learned while reading *Bleak House* during rehab. To me probate meant rainy London streets, courts of Chancery, and interminably long hearings about the distribution of estates—hearings which eventually resulted in the lawyers getting all the money. Portland had many a rainy street. Courts still sat in equity, that peculiar arm of law which does without juries and the other annoyances of citizen participation. The probate court in downtown Portland was close enough to Chancery for me, and I didn't object to mind-numbing cases about other people's money as long as I got a reasonable chunk of it in the end.

My home life was simple. Three years into my last suspension my third wife got fed up and ran off with my car mechanic. I called up Don Yerke, the titular boss of Lawyers Helping Lawyers, a support group for lawyers recovering from alcoholism. Despite the fact that I was drinking at the time he steered me to a second floor flat in a lime green Victorian down by the Willamette River. The riverfront on the east side of Portland was the warehouse district, but fifty years earlier it had been a thriving residential community. Quite a few crumbling Victorian walk-ups still survived in the nooks and crannies after light industry and warehousing had pushed out the families. The place Yerke got me was sandwiched between a mattress factory and a print shop. Out my front bay window I could watch the loading dock of Haven Appliance, a wholesaler of appliance parts, or the comings and goings at Avian House, some sort of fraternal organization that seemed to have run out of members. I liked the apartment mostly for the sounds. I could hear the freeway traffic from my bedroom window. The big trucks arriving early in the morning rattled my windows. I like the sound of cities.

The only other place in my life was Murdock's. Murdock's was the AA group closest to my apartment.

It was Hal's Place without the alcohol. After graduating rehab, I had to find an AA meeting where I could get those slips signed to prove to the Bar that I was staying sober. There were a lot of clean respectable places I could have gone to do that. Murdock's was not one of them.

Murdock's held its meetings in a run down rented storefront about half a mile from my apartment. The group got its name from John Murdock, a man who decades earlier had started the group among the homeless drunks and addicts who slept in the doorways of Portland's skid road.

Murdock's wasn't listed in the official directory of Portland's AA meetings. Real AA in Portland didn't want to admit that the place existed and the people at Murdock's liked it that way. One Saturday in the days after rehab, but before the Bar had given me my license back, I was taking a morning constitutional through the warehouse district and encountered the AA symbol on the door with the words, "This is the door you have been looking for." People were going in so I followed and took a seat in the back. Having been sentenced to AA several different times over the years, I had seen a lot of it. What happened at Murdock's was different.

The AA I had been used to in the church basements and community centers was a cheery AA with a lot of hand holding, hugging, and loving people until they could learn to love themselves. The people at Murdock's weren't like that. The people at Murdock's were mean.

At Murdock's, the book *Alcoholics Anonymous* was the meat and potatoes of every meeting. The chairman read aloud from the book and when he got the urge, would call on someone to speak. The speakers never used "My name is Whatever and I am an alcoholic" for an introduction, and if the speaker bothered to identify him or herself at all there was no chorus of "Hi Whatever" from the audience. People did not applaud. People didn't hug or hold hands. It was a place where you could sit in a crowded room and still be alone.

I went to Murdock's my required three times a week to listen and get my slips signed. By that damp autumn of 2005 I had been going there enough to recognize the regulars and not get glared at when I came in late and took a seat in the back. Most of the people at Murdock's were society's rejects: ex-criminals, ex-cops, and all manner of people who identified themselves by what they used to be. Mental illness was as welcome as alcoholism. The members of Murdock's didn't claim their program could cure depression or schizophrenia, but believed that the mentally ill were better off sober than drunk.

So when Churley Dowd told me his wife's name, I smiled. The time I had spent with Daisy Twill had been in AA meetings at Murdock's.